John Watson

Christianity and Idealism

Vol. 1

John Watson

Christianity and Idealism
Vol. 1

ISBN/EAN: 9783337101565

Printed in Europe, USA, Canada, Australia, Japan

Cover: Foto ©Lupo / pixelio.de

More available books at **www.hansebooks.com**

CHRISTIANITY AND IDEALISM

THE CHRISTIAN IDEAL OF LIFE IN ITS RELATIONS
TO THE GREEK AND JEWISH IDEALS AND
TO MODERN PHILOSOPHY

BY

JOHN WATSON, LL.D.
PROFESSOR OF MORAL PHILOSOPHY IN QUEEN'S UNIVERSITY
KINGSTON, CANADA

New York
THE MACMILLAN COMPANY
LONDON: MACMILLAN & CO., LTD.
1897

All rights reserved

CONTENTS

	PAGE
NOTE BY THE EDITOR	vii
INTRODUCTORY PREFACE	xxi

PART I

THE CHRISTIAN IDEAL OF LIFE IN RELATION TO THE GREEK AND JEWISH IDEALS

CHAPTER I

HISTORICAL CONNEXION OF MORALITY AND RELIGION . 1

CHAPTER II

THE GREEK IDEAL 23

CHAPTER III

THE JEWISH IDEAL 45

CHAPTER IV

THE CHRISTIAN IDEAL . . . 60

CHAPTER V

MEDIÆVAL CHRISTIANITY . . . 110

Part II

MODERN IDEALISM IN ITS RELATION TO THE CHRISTIAN IDEAL OF LIFE

CHAPTER VI

General Statement and Defence of Idealism . . 121

CHAPTER VII

Idealism in relation to Agnosticism and the Special Sciences 153

CHAPTER VIII

Idealism and Christianity 192

NOTE BY THE EDITOR

THE present volume, though the first to come from the press, is in its proper order the second in a series of publications projected by the Philosophical Union of the University of California. The first volume, entitled *The Conception of God*, by Professor Royce of Harvard University and a number of his critics, has been thrown out of its natural place by the stress of circumstances, but will presently be issued, and in due time will be followed by others from various writers of philosophical weight. Each volume in the series will in a manner represent the culmination of a group of studies prosecuted by the Union, usually during an academic year; it will consist, mainly, of the contribution made to those studies by some thinker of note whose previous writings have formed the nucleus of the year's work, and who comes at the invitation of the Union to take in person the chief and concluding part in the work.

The society whose pursuits are to result in these publications contains members of nearly every shade of current philosophical opinion: the positivist, the agnostic, the unsettled inquirer, all have their free expression and hearing in it, as well as the idealist of nearly every type. It is true, however, that the dominant tone of the Union is affirmative and idealistic. The decided majority of its members are animated by a conviction that human thought is able to solve the riddle of life *positively;* to solve it in accord with the ideal hopes and interests of human nature. They are convinced that, for better or worse, enlightened mankind has in matters of belief taken a final leave of mere tradition and of blank authority, — of miraculism in every form. It is accordingly clear to them that the only safety for human practice henceforth, the practice of each or the practice of all, lies in founding it on a philosophic criticism that shall be luminous, unrelenting, penetrating to the bottom, and that yet, just because of this unsparing thoroughness, will affirm the reality of all those moral beliefs and religious hopes on which the achievements of western civilisation have hitherto rested, and by the undermining of which the stability of society now threatens to give way.

A certain thread of continuity, coming from this affirmative aim, is discernible in the writings that form the first two volumes in the proposed series. Indeed, this is obvious from their titles — *The Conception of God* and *Christianity and Idealism*. Were one to say that a logical march seems manifest here, as if there were an advance from the question of Theism in general to the more specific question of Christian Theism, the statement would not be incorrect. Such a line in the discussion, such an advance in it along the historical course of religious belief, has actually been in mind. It corresponds, too, to the course of attack upon the ideals of past culture which the negative philosophical criticism in our century has taken. That attack has accustomed us to the repeated sceptical questions: Is there any proof that there is even a God? Is there any, at all events, that Christianity is true? Are we any longer Theists, even? In any case, are we any longer Christians? A philosophical procedure aiming to affirm the reality of the ideal elements in our achieved civilisation would naturally follow the path of these questions, and, by a critical appreciation at once of their supports and of their limits, would pass to the justification of a rational Theism, and onward to that of a rational Christianity.

The present volume thus has for its theme the interdependence of Christianity and Idealism; of Christianity regarded, not as historical theology, but as an ideal of conduct, and Idealism so stated as to become, in the author's conviction, completely self-consistent, and thus expressive of a reason completely self-critical. Professor Watson argues, tacitly, that Christianity and Idealism, when each is duly understood, lend each other a stable support. From this point of view, no doubt, a large part of historical theology called

Christian will fall away, even of that which has been regarded as of the essence of Christianity, and Christianity will be seen as in its truth the new but abiding principle of personal and social action that marked a fresh and higher stage in human development, and that amid all foreign surroundings or accretions has ever since been the real prime mover in the progress of civilisation. On the other hand, Idealism, responding to a like logic, will assume the form proper to it as simply the philosophical expression of whatever is most characteristic of man in his animation by rational ideals. In this common light each will prove the other true; for each will be seen to be but a different expression of the same indivisibly threefold Fact — God, human responsible freedom, and human immortality. Idealism will prove to be nothing more nor less than the principle of morality and religion on the one hand, the principle of advancing history on the other, in their comprehended fulfilment; while Christianity, now discerned in its essence, distinguished from its accidental embodiments and encumbrances, will be seen to be that in germ which Idealism is in full issue. Both get in this way the vast and impressive sanction that attaches to everything structural in the growth of history. Neither can any longer be viewed as an accident or a caprice, but both are discovered to be intrinsic in things as things historically are; both to be aspects of that Reason which is the reality of the real, both constitutive in the Reality which is rational through and through. Necessary to this massive style of proof, would be an exhibition of Christianity in its historical development out of and above earlier religions, especially Judaism and Hellenism, and an exposition of Idealism as rising out of and over lower philosophies, surmounting in logically natural sequence Empiricism, Positivism, Agnosticism, and the successive inchoate or arrested forms of its own doctrine. To this course of argument the plan of the present work, as set forth in its successive parts and their chapters, manifestly corresponds.

The book forms a natural sequel to its author's previous work *Comte, Mill, and Spencer*, and, though in its second part beginning like that with a polemic against the sceptical and agnostic factors in the thinking of these writers and of Kant, seeks to bring into view the deep affirmative implication, the larger Idealism, that forms the silent presupposition of their reasoning, however little suspected by them. Directed upon the negative thought so prevalent in our century, both works aim to re-establish the human values invaded by it, not by thrusting it out as worthless, but through supplementing it by the larger affirmation which at once gives to the negative its relative justification, its function in the reasoned total truth, and yet exposes the one-sidedness that would recognise it exclusively. It was in view of this pertinence to the mental situation of the times, that the Union made the *Comte, Mill, and Spencer* the basis of its studies for the year 1895–96, submitted the criticism advanced in the book to a counter-criticism by such of its members as might fairly lay claim to expert knowledge in the various sciences concerned — mathematics, physics, biology, the theory of evolution, the history of philosophy — and invited the author to visit the Union from his distant home, to complete his part of the discussion in a series of lectures. The result is the book before us.

The reader, however, would be insecure in assuming that because the new work is issued at the instance of the Union, the philosophy set forth in it is regarded by the members as a final solution of the grave questions agitating our times. Certainly, the most active and influential of them are in strong sympathy with the general position of its author: belief in our responsible freedom, in our immortality, and in God, they regard as lying at the foundation of civilised society, and they think its defence is only achievable through some form of Idealism. But many of them, and among these the present writer, are impressed with the difficulty under which all philosophy labours since Kant, in the effort to reach the complete ideal desired — the inseparably correlated truths of God, real human freedom, and immortality genuinely personal. The clue to this threefold union of truths is fastened in human free-agency, comprehended as meaning self-activity profoundly inward and unqualifiedly real; and the difficulty lies in seeing how the conception of an immanent God, joined with the seeming impossibility of proving any other God on Kantian principles of knowledge, can be consistent with such freedom. Those of us who are convinced of this inconsistency are therefore looking for another way with Idealism; we believe that the time has perhaps arrived when this other way can be opened, and a new philosophical departure begun. This is not the place, of course, to set forth its method; let the mere hint suffice, that, for its starting-point, we shall look to a renewed criticism of Kant, addressed primarily to closing the gap which he left between the Practical and the Theoretical Reason, and to establishing an effective instead of a merely nominal primacy of the former over the latter: it would be shown, namely, that the moral and religious consciousness, with its postulate of a world of Persons, really free, enters as a constitutive condition into the possibility of the world of sense-perception itself, and is thus the finally determining factor in the logic of nature and of predictive natural science. In this way the world of the moral and religious consciousness would be embraced in the complete and genuine world of science; knowledge directed upon nature would be shown to be only one special function of intelligence, and the world of absolute realities would be recovered for the intellect.

To those who may feel that the reconciliation of human freedom with the literal immanence of the Divine Being is more than human wit can compass, it may be well to point out that this is the only conception of God left possible by Kant for minds who accept his *Analytic*, with its necessary "schematism" of the Categories, limiting knowledge to the range of possible experience, and who still would lay hold on God by knowledge rather than by unsupported faith. If the tenet of Kant is to stand, that no knowledge is possible unless the knowing subject and the known object fall within one and the same self-consciousness, then the God of knowledge must be this immanent God, and human freedom must make the best of it. But *will* the tenet stand?—*must* it stand? It is in direct contradiction with that other tenet, Kant's very starting-point: That a perceptive consciousness implies, unmistakably, some reality other than its own. Which of the two tenets is to reign and to endure? To us of the Union who look for the new way with Idealism, these are the signal questions for the future of philosophy. To minds at a loss to find a God knowable and yet compatible with their freedom, or, in other terms, with their genuine reality, our word would be: Return to Kant's critical starting-point, follow his critical method by interpreting the necessary transcendent object in the light of Practical Reason, but do this with critical consistency; at one stroke, give his foundation-tenet a logical footing and refute his opposing tenet, by showing that his world of the Practical Reason, the world of real Persons, is a condition of the possibility of perception itself, if this is to be *objective* and not a mere experience — a mere state of the particular subject. There is no conceivable criterion by which an experience could be discriminated as objective, except the consenting judgment of a total society of minds.

But, differ as they may from the author, if indeed they do differ, the members of the Union are happy in being the agents of giving to the world a writing of his that has the solid philosophical worth which they believe the present work possesses. After all, and in these times of fundamental doubt especially, one of the greatest philosophical services is to rouse men to a thoroughly critical search into the whole course of serious thought and its meaning, and to do this in the only effective way — by exhibiting the encouraging truth that it *has* a meaning, that its earnest efforts cannot end in mere scepticism, indifference, or despair. We offer this book to the reader, confident of the secure wisdom of its author's sentence: " The failures of successive philosophies are not in any sense absolute; with each step in advance, the problem becomes clearer and more easy of solution." We believe, too, that the work has a live relation to the questions most urgent just now. These amount to no less than this: either the entire abandonment of the moral and religious conceptions upon which the culture of our western nations has been bred, or else the preservation of their living heart despite the free stripping away of the coverings in which they have been protected and nourished. It is all-important that belief in this living heart of Christianity shall be rationally preserved, and that in the process of casting off its foreign and outworn integuments its vital substance shall neither be lost, impaired, nor adulterated. To repeat the language of the lamented author of *Literature and Dogma*, "An inevitable revolution, of which we all recognise the beginnings and the signs, but which has already spread, perhaps, farther than most of us think, is befalling the religion in which we have been brought up"; and, amid its course, the greatest need of the times is a deep and accurate definition of Christianity as it really is, when its belief is stated in the highest and simplest terms, pure yet sufficing. For lack of this, Arnold's own effort to take advantage of the tide in this religious revolution proved to be too great a yielding to the prevailing current of scepticism; the distinction between his "Eternal, not ourselves, that makes for righteousness" and the "Unknowable" of the agnostic became so attenuated as to be without practical significance, and in abandoning the personality, sacrificed the vital quality of God. The present work, by its comprehensive yet luminous interpretation of the teaching of Jesus, and its organic connecting of this with the highest philosophic insights, we believe goes far toward settling the desired definition as it is. For this reason, we feel that it will meet a profoundly real want in all earnest and quickened minds, and we send it forth with a large and hopeful confidence.

G. H. HOWISON.

UNIVERSITY OF CALIFORNIA, BERKELEY,
October 27, 1896.

INTRODUCTORY PREFACE

THE present work has grown out of lectures recently delivered before the Philosophical Union of the University of California. What is called Part I. is the expansion of a lecture on "The Greek and Christian Ideals of Life," and the remainder contains the substance of two lectures in defence of Idealism, with a good deal of additional matter.

The historical matter of the first part does not pretend to be a complete presentation of the development of religion. It was my first intention to attempt such a presentation, but I soon found that it was impossible to compress so abundant a material within the limits assigned to me, and I have therefore confined myself to a statement of the general course of religious development, with a more particular consideration of the Greek and Jewish ideals of life, as compared with the

Christian. In treating of these topics, I have avoided all polemical discussion, aiming rather to give the results of many years of reading and reflection, than to occupy space with a consideration of conflicting views. The chapter on the Christian Ideal is based upon a study of the synoptic gospels, as read in the light of modern historical and philosophical criticism. Here, above all, it seemed advisable to avoid as far as possible all purely doctrinal topics, concentrating attention entirely upon the conception of life which may be, as I think, constructed from the sayings of Jesus himself. I am by no means indifferent to the development by theologians of the fundamental ideas of the Founder of Christianity, but it seems to me that the wonderful power and persuasiveness of those ideas is most apparent when they are exhibited in their naked purity.

It seems almost necessary to say a word or two upon the use of the term "Idealism." The objection has been raised that no school of thought has an exclusive right to the title. In answer to this objection perhaps I cannot do better than try to explain why I think the term "Idealism" may be fairly employed to designate the general theory which is here advocated.

I presume it will be admitted that the originator of the philosophical doctrine of Idealism was Plato, and that Plato conceived of the first principle of all things as reason (Νοῦς), also maintaining that it is in virtue of reason, as distinguished from sensible perception, that man obtains a knowledge of that principle. Now, modern Idealism, as I understand it, agrees with Plato on these two points, and therefore its claim to the name does not seem either arrogant or unreasonable. No system has a right to call itself "idealistic," in the Platonic sense, which does not in some form accept the doctrine of the rationality and knowability of the real. Applying this test, we must exclude Agnosticism, which denies that we can know the real as it is in itself; Scepticism, which refuses to admit that we can make any absolute affirmation whatever, either positive or negative; and Sensationalism or Empiricism, which finds in the sensible and its customary modes of conjunction the only knowable world. To call by the name of Idealism, as is sometimes done, a doctrine which reduces all knowable reality to individual states or feelings, is surely an unwarrantable use of the term.

If it is said that, interpreted in the wide sense here given to it, Idealism must include systems differing so greatly as those of Descartes and Hegel, or of Spinoza and Lotze, I entirely agree. The systems of Descartes, Spinoza, Leibnitz, Kant, Fichte, Schelling, Hegel, and Lotze all seem to me to be forms of Idealism, and the only question is how far any of them can claim to be true to the principle that "the real is rational." The test, therefore, of an idealistic philosophy is its ability to provide a system of ideas which shall best harmonise with the principle upon which Idealism is based; or, rather, the success of an idealistic philosophy must consist in its ability to prove that "the real is rational," and that man is capable of knowing it to be rational. I am very far from affirming that the hurried sketch of an idealistic philosophy here presented fulfils that demand: all that is attempted is to expose the irrelevancy of certain objections which have been made from a misunderstanding of what Idealism affirms, and to indicate the main line of thought which it must follow, and the main conclusions to which it leads.

It may help to indicate the points in which Idealism, as here presented, differs from some of the great historical forms which it has assumed, if I state wherein these seem to be defective. In doing so, it will not be possible to enter into detail, or to support by reasoned proof the conclusions to which I have been led. I shall therefore have to assume a general acquaintance with the history of philosophy on the part of the reader, and I beg him to take the criticisms which I shall make simply as results, the evidence for which I hope to give in detail on another occasion.

Plato may be called the Father of Idealism, though, no doubt, his doctrine was a development from the Idealism implied in the Νοῦς of Anaxagoras, and still more clearly in the Socratic view of universals. How far, then, may it be said that Plato was untrue to his central idea of the rationality and knowability of the real? His main defect, as it seems to me, was in virtually opposing the real to the actual or so-called "sensible." This defect is obvious in his theory, or one of his theories, that Art consists in the "imitation" of ordinary "sensible" actuality. The similar defect in his Philosophy of Religion it will not be necessary to exhibit here, as I have dealt with it in the body of the work; but a word may be said in regard to his defective Theory of Knowledge. Just as Plato at last rejects Art on the ground that it only represents or imitates the "sensible," so he shows a decided tendency to separate the universal from the particular. He does, indeed, maintain that whatever is real must be self-active; but in separating reason, as it exists in us, from sensible perception, he virtually empties reason of all content, and makes its objects pure abstractions.

The philosophy of Aristotle is beset by similar defects, though in him the contrast of the real or ideal and the actual is less rigid and is more obviously in process of being transcended. Like Plato, he starts from the "mimetic" theory of Art, but he is led to make assertions which are contradictory of his starting-point. Thus he virtually asserts (1) that Art is such an interpretation of the actual as serves to bring out its deeper meaning, (2) that it gives rise to a feeling of self-harmony, and (3) that its object is spiritual forces in their deepest reality. Yet, since he never abandoned the view that Art is an "imitation" of the sensible, it cannot be said that he attained to a self-consistent theory. The reason for this discrepancy comes to light in his Philosophy of Religion, where he does not get beyond the idea of God as a self-centred Being, and is therefore forced to conceive of the world as related to God in an external or arbitrary way. Similarly, in his Theory of Knowledge, he shrinks from the admission that the actual is rational. There is always in things, as he thinks, a recalcitrant element or "matter," which is the source of "contingency" or "chance." It is not merely that human knowledge cannot completely comprehend the actual, but the actual is itself imperfect, and therefore the ideal "forms" as they exist for the divine reason, being entirely free from "matter," are essentially different from the actual, in which "form" is always more or less sunk in "matter."

When we pass from ancient to modern philosophy, we find the same problem of the reconciliation of the real and the actual confronting us; but the antagonism seems more difficult of solution, because the contrast of the finite and the infinite has been sharpened by the explicit claim of the individual to accept nothing which does not commend itself to his reason.

By Descartes, two opposite methods are employed,— the method of abstraction and the method of definition. In the use of the former, he is led to maintain that the only permanent or unchanging attribute of body is geometrical extension; in employing the latter, he assumes that there are a number of real things, each having a definite or limited amount of extension. Spinoza turns the former view against the latter, pointing out that there is nothing in the idea of pure extension which entitles us to conceive of it as broken up into parts. There can therefore, he argues, be no individual bodies, but only a single substance without parts or limits. Leibnitz, again, agrees with Spinoza in holding that pure space has no limits, but the inference he draws is that space is not an attribute of real substance, but a pure abstraction, derived from our experience of the order which obtains among the confused objects of sense. Thus all the spatial determinations of things, as merely confused ideas, have no existence from the point of view of thought; a view which converts the actual into pure illusion.

To Descartes it seemed that the human mind cannot comprehend the ends which God must be supposed to have in creation, and therefore he maintained that we must give up the vain search for final causes. "All God's ends are hidden in the inscrutable abyss of his wisdom." Descartes, however, tacitly assumed that there are such ends, if only we could discover them. Such a doctrine is manifestly self-contradictory, and therefore Spinoza was only following out this side of the Cartesian doctrine to its logical result when he denied final causes altogether. Leibnitz, on the other hand, refused to admit that human knowledge is limited to the orderly movements of nature, as both Descartes and Spinoza assumed, and therefore he maintained that, without the idea of final cause, or activity directed towards an end, we cannot explain the world at all. We must therefore conceive of every real being or "monad" as self-active and purposive. Each "monad" is ever striving to make explicit what is already contained obscurely in it, and each "represents" the whole world from its own point of view, so that all "monads," without any actual connexion with one another, harmonise in their perceptions. Now (a) it is a pure assumption that there are absolutely independent "monads," in which there already exists obscurely all that afterwards comes to more or less clear expression; an assumption which has no better warrant than the preconception that identity is incompatible with development. (*b*) It is equally an assumption that each monad "represents" the world. On the Leibnitzian hypothesis of purely individual beings, each shut up within itself, there can be no way of proving that there is any world to "represent." The only real individuality, as I should maintain, is that of a being which knows itself because it knows other beings. (*c*) When he comes to explain the "harmony" of the monads with one another, Leibnitz has to fall back upon the idea of the selective activity of the divine will. Out of all the possible worlds which lay before the divine mind, that was chosen which was the best on the whole. Here, therefore, in the final result of the Leibnitzian philosophy, we see the fundamental discrepancy which vitiates his whole system. The actual world after all is not rational, but only as rational as God could make it; a theory which leaves us no ground for inferring the rationality of God at all, but on the contrary presupposes an absolute limit in the divine mind. Thus the Idealism of Leibnitz, suggestive as it is, ultimately breaks down in contradiction. Can we, then, accept the Critical Idealism of Kant?

I cannot do more here than indicate the defects in the philosophy of Kant which prevent us from regarding it as final. Its fundamental imperfection is the abstract opposition of the empirical and the ideal, as if the former were not implicitly the latter. This opposition meets us first in his theory of knowledge, in which a virtual contrast is drawn between what is knowable and what lies beyond the boundaries of knowledge. Such a contrast is ultimately unmeaning. The only reality by reference to which we can criticise the knowable world of ordinary experience is a reality which includes, though it further elucidates, that world. Failing to recognise this truth, the philosophy of Kant is vexed by the perpetual recurrence of self-contradiction in some new form, a self-contradiction which is never finally transcended. (1) In the *Æsthetic*, Kant adopts the compromise, that space and time belong to the subject, while individual things in space and time are relative to an unknown object. But, as these individuals must enter into knowledge, he is compelled to regard the unknown object as a mere blank, and such an object cannot be contrasted with anything; it is, in fact, merely the known world stripped of its determinateness and hypostatised. Kant is here really criticising the known world by an abstract phase of itself, and pronouncing the former to be lower instead of higher than the latter. The pure object can only be regarded as higher than the known world, in so far as the spatial and temporal world is seen to be a lower form of the knowable world. In this sense, no doubt, we may say that the undefined object, or thing in itself, indicates the world as it exists in idea, *i.e.* the world as completely determined. (2) In the *Analytic*, Kant takes another step in the process by which he gives a higher meaning to the thing in itself. The *whole* of the knowable world is now shown to involve the unifying activity of the knowing subject, though with the reservation that the object is conceived as the source of the undefined "manifold of sense." But, in truth, there is no undefined "manifold" *for knowledge*, and hence the thing in itself is, even more palpably than before, a *magni nominis umbra*. (3) This is partly recognised by Kant himself when he goes on to consider the Unconditioned in its three forms,—the soul, the world, and God. (*a*) His criticism of Rational Psychology is virtually a recognition of the truth, that the pure or unrelated subject is a mere fiction of abstraction. Yet he does not draw the proper inference, that the real subject exists only in and through its relations to the object. Such a subject is not mechanically determinable, being self-conscious and self-active, but it does not and could not exist, were not the system of nature what it is. (*b*) Kant's criticism of Rational Cosmology is valid, so far as it points out that the reflective understanding seeks to affirm one of two related terms as if they were mutually exclusive; but Kant does not see that the reconciliation of these opposites is possible without recourse being had to the unknowable region of "noumena." (*c*) The criticism of Rational Theology is valid as against the dualistic separation of being and thought, the world and God; but Kant's own solution is inadequate, because he regards these oppositions as holding absolutely within the sphere of the knowable, whereas they are really oppositions which carry their own refutation with them.

When he passes from the Theoretical to the Practical Reason, Kant at last recognises that the self-conscious subject is synthetic or productive; in other words, that here the real object is not opposed to the subject as something unintelligible, but, on the contrary, is bound up with the very nature of the subject. But the shadow of the "thing in itself" still haunts him, and therefore he conceives this objective world as merely an ideal which demands realisation, but which can never be realised. The way out of this difficulty is to recognise that the ideal *is* the real: that morality is not a mere "beyond," but is actually realised objectively in human institutions, which themselves have permanence only as they are in harmony with the eternal nature of the world, or, in other words, with the nature of God.

In the *Critique of Judgment* Kant makes a final effort to overcome the dualism with which he started. In æsthetic feeling he finds a sort of unconscious testimony to the unity of the phenomenal and the real, and in organised beings he meets with a phase of things which refuses to come under the head either of the phenomenal or the noumenal. Thus, "as by a side gesture," Kant points beyond the abstractions of the sensible and the supersensible to their actual concrete unity; but the preconception with which he started prevents him from identifying the ideal and the real, and the most he can persuade himself to say is, that man is entitled to a rational *faith* in God, freedom and immortality, though these are objects which lie beyond the range of his *knowledge*.

I should be sorry if what has been said should suggest the idea that philosophy is merely a series of brilliant failures, in which each new thinker vainly strives to prove the unprovable proposition, that the actual world when properly understood is rational; rather, as it seems to me, faith in the rationality of the universe is the incentive and presupposition of all philosophical progress. Nor are the failures of successive philosophies in any case absolute; with each step in advance the problem becomes clearer and more easy of solution. How far the outline of Idealism contained in the second part of this essay is free from the objections which I have tried to indicate, must be left for the reader to determine. Perhaps I may venture to say that, if it has any special value, that value lies in the attempt to reconcile the reality of individual things, and especially the freedom and individuality of man, with the fundamental principle of Idealism, that the actual properly understood is a manifestation in various degree of one self-conscious and self-determining spiritual Being.

It would be difficult to enumerate all the books to which I have been directly or indirectly indebted, especially in the preparation of the first part of this essay; but I must not omit to mention the various works of the Master of Balliol, and of Professor Pfleiderer, as well as Leopold Schmidt's *Die*

Ethik der alten Griechen, Mr. Jebb's *Growth and Influence of Classical Greek Poetry*, with the introductions in his edition of Sophocles, Mr. Bosanquet's *History of Æsthetic*, Dr. Driver's *Introduction to the Literature of the Old Testament* and *Isaiah*, Weber's *System der altsynagogalen palästinischen Theologie*, Schürer's *History of the Jewish People*, Keim's *Jesus of Nazara*, and Weizsäcker's *Das Apostolische Zeitalter*. In preparing the chapter on the Christian Ideal I also received valuable assistance from my colleague, Professor Macnaughton.

JOHN WATSON.

QUEEN'S UNIVERSITY, KINGSTON, CANADA,
    October 1, 1896.

PART I

THE CHRISTIAN IDEAL OF LIFE IN RELATION TO THE GREEK AND JEWISH IDEALS

THE CHRISTIAN IDEAL OF LIFE

CHAPTER I

HISTORICAL CONNEXION OF MORALITY AND RELIGION

Christianity, as it issued fresh from the mind of its founder, embodied a conception of life which brought religion into indissoluble connexion with morality. The whole human race was conceived of as in idea a single spiritual organism, in which each man gains his own perfection by self-conscious identification with all the rest, and this community of life was held to be possible only because man is identical in nature, though not in person, with the one divine principle which is manifested in all forms of being. Man, it was therefore held, is unable to come to unity with himself until he has surrendered his whole being to the influence of the Holy Spirit. On this view there is no basis for the moral ideal, and no possibility of its realisation, apart from the religious ideal; for man cannot accept as the standard of his life an ideal which is not in absolute harmony with the ultimate principle of the universe; nor, even if he did, could his effort to realise it be anything but the struggle with an alien power too strong for him, — a struggle as futile as the attempt of the Teutonic giant of the northern Saga to lift the deep-seated earth from its foundations. Affirming that the life of man is moral, just in so far as it is in harmony with the divine nature, Christianity rests upon the belief that "goodness is the nature of things," and therefore it maintains that evil, which it regards as positive and antagonistic to good, exists in order to be transcended, and must succumb to the all-conquering power of goodness. Accordingly, man's religious faith, which alone gives meaning to his moral effort, is for the individual the source of a joyous consciousness of unity with himself, just because in overcoming the world he overcomes his own lower self. It is true that the evil which exists without and within him can never be completely abolished, but it is always in process of being abolished; and therefore the Christian is enabled to preserve his optimism even in face of the worst forms of evil.

No one will deny that in this triumphant faith Jesus and his first followers lived, but the objection may be raised, that the simple faith of an earlier age is not possible for us in these days, or at least not until the doubts and perplexities, which the facts of experience, the results of science, and the deepened reflection of our time inevitably suggest, have been fairly weighed and resolved. The wounds of reflection, it may be said, are too deep to be healed by a childlike faith in God and man, which rests rather upon sentiment than upon rational evidence. Many will go even further, and maintain that morality not only *can*, but *must*, be divorced from religion, and that in any case it does not depend for its support upon any form of religious belief.

Various reasons may be given for this separation of morality from religion, but they will all be found to rest ultimately on the assumption that it is not possible for man, with his limited faculties and knowledge, to get behind the veil of phenomena and grasp reality as it is in itself. Thus the real becomes simply a name for that which lies beyond the range of our finite vision, and morality is therefore conceived as merely that course of conduct which we must adopt in order to make the most of the circumstances in which we happen to be placed. So firm a hold has this doctrine taken of the modern mind, that not merely those who reject Christianity, but even some of its professed champions, such as Mr. Balfour, regard moral ideas as the only foundation upon which even a "provisional theory" of life can be based; and we even find Browning, in one of his moods, suggesting that the limitation of knowledge is essential to the stability and progress of morality.

An attempt will be made, in the second part of this essay, to show that religion and morality cannot be separated from each other without the destruction of both, and that the essential identity of the human and divine natures, which is the central idea of Christianity, is the legitimate result of philosophical reflection. Meantime, it may be pointed out that the whole history of man goes to show that the connexion of morality with religion is so close that no advance in the one has ever taken place without a corresponding advance in the other. What is distinctive of Christianity is not the union of morality with religion, but the comprehensiveness of the principle upon which that union is based. Every religion embodies the highest ideal of a people, and the morality which corresponds to it is the special form in which that ideal is sought to be realised. It follows that, when the religious ideal is no longer an adequate expression of the more developed consciousness of a people, the moral ideal is also perceived to be in need of revision. Thus the history of religion is inseparable from the history of morality.

That religion and morality have, as a matter of fact, always been connected in the closest way, might be proved by a detailed examination of the whole history of religion; but, as the proof would lead us too far afield, one or two instances where the connexion seems at first sight to be broken will have to suffice.

(1) It has been maintained that in early times religion had nothing to do with morality. That this view is untenable, it will not be difficult to show. One of the earliest forms of religion is the belief in a god or totem, who is at once some being lower than man, and yet is regarded as the ancestor of a particular family or tribe. The theory of Mr. Spencer, that this form of religion originated in the worship of ancestors and was afterwards developed into totemism, cannot be accepted, because it assumes that primitive man was at a higher stage of development than his descendants. If primitive man was able to draw a clear distinction between himself and lower forms of being, it is inconceivable that his descendants should

have seen no fundamental distinction between them. The truth seems to be that the totem, which is almost always a plant, an animal, or other natural object, is viewed as divine because it forms the medium for that haunting sense of something incomprehensible and therefore divine, of which even early man is not entirely destitute. The totem is the form in which this feeling is objectified, and it then becomes the vehicle for the ideal union of the family or tribe. Thus the religion of early man is bound up with the elementary moral ideas which rule his life. The only social bond of which he can conceive is that of the family or tribe. Moreover, the members of each family or tribe, while they are closely related to one another, are usually hostile to other families or tribes; and hence the morality which corresponds to this phase of religion is based upon hatred of all who fall beyond its limited range. Here, therefore, the correspondence of religion and morality is obvious: a religion in which the object of worship is viewed as the ancestor of a certain stock naturally goes with a form of morality which involves hatred of the members of all other stocks. This hatred, as it is inseparable from the moral ideas of early man, finds its expression in his religion: and hence the totems of other families or tribes are regarded as evil spirits, whose baneful influence can be counteracted only by cunning and magical spells.

(2) Perhaps it may be conceded that the morality of early man is a faithful reflex of his religion, but it may be held that their connexion is dissolved when an advance has been made to a more developed form of society. It is easy to understand that, in the earlier stages of human history, whatever is sanctioned by religion should be blindly followed; but at a more advanced stage, when reflection begins to claim its rights, it may seem that progress in morality is rather hindered than aided by religion. Was it religion, it may be asked, which led in Greece to the higher morality of the age of Pericles? Would it not be truer to say that the religion of Greece was far behind its morality, and offered a stubborn resistance to its progress?

"The Greek poets," as Mr. Max Müller says, "had an instinctive aversion to anything excessive or monstrous, yet they would relate of their gods what would make the most savage of Red Indians creep and shudder." Does not this fact clearly show that morality advances independently of religion, and may even be in conflict with it?

The answer to this argument for the separation of morality and religion is not far to seek. The moral ideas of the age of Pericles were no doubt antagonistic to the older religious ideas preserved in Greek mythology, but they were in perfect harmony with the religious ideas which really ruled the best minds. The sanctity which attaches to religion long preserves traditional forms of belief from being openly assailed, but this is quite consistent with a transformation of the whole spirit of the earlier faith. In estimating the character of a religion we must in all cases make allowance for the survival of ideas which have lost their power and meaning, and concentrate our attention upon the new content which is preserved in the old earthen vessels. The application of this principle, which is universal in its range, is in the present case obvious. The Greek religion, like the religion of every progressive people, was in continuous process of development; but in its later phases it retained elements which, though they were not explicitly rejected, occupied a very subordinate place and were practically ignored. The real religious beliefs of Greece in the age of Pericles were embodied, not in its mythology, but in the interpretation of the legends given by Pindar, Æschylus, and Sophocles. When this is once seen, it becomes obvious that the religion of Greece, so far from being at any time on a lower plane than its morality, was in all cases an expression of the highest ideal of which the Greek was capable, an ideal which he was seeking to realise in the various forms of his social life.

(3) As the morality of Greece seems at first sight to be in advance of its religion, so it may appear that the religious ideal of the Jews is entirely divorced from their moral conceptions. The continual refrain of their

great prophets, especially those of the eighth century, is that Israel, while she accepts the lofty ideal of God revealed long ago to their fathers, has, in practice, forsaken the Lord, and is governed by the lowest ethical ideal. When, however, we penetrate beneath the form of the prophetic utterances, it becomes obvious that the Jews are no exception to the rule that the moral and religious ideas of a people are the precise counterpart of each other. The Jewish prophet refers the higher conception of God, with which he is himself inspired, to an original revelation given by God to his people in the past, while in truth that conception has been gradually evolved out of a lower and cruder form of faith. It is no doubt true that the religious ideal upon which he insists is far in advance of the moral ideas of his time, but it is equally in advance of its religious ideas. The mass of the Jewish people had never freed themselves from the earlier idea of a tribal god who was gracious to Israel and terrible to her enemies; and hence their morality was not in harmony with that ideal of an absolutely holy God, "of purer eyes than to behold iniquity," which had disclosed itself in the higher consciousness of the prophets. The religious conceptions of the Jewish people as a whole were, therefore, in entire harmony with their moral conceptions. The contradiction is not between a pure and lofty religion and a low moral ideal, but between the lower ideal, religious and moral, beyond which the people had not advanced, and the higher ideal embodied in the prophetic utterances. It is no doubt a radical distinction between the Greek and the Jewish religion, that the former was simply an idealised transcript of society as it actually existed, while the latter, in its higher form, was a picture of a righteous kingdom that was placed in some far-off future; but this distinction, important as it is, does not imply that the Jewish religion created a divorce between the ideal and the actual. For, though the prophets continually speak of a time when Israel shall "return" to the Lord, this "return" is in reality an advance to a higher form of religion and morality. The ideal of the future is always conceived to consist in a religious reformation which will manifest itself in a moral regeneration; and though, at a very late age, the hope of deliverance from outward and inward evil by a natural process of development had been lost, the Jewish mind never entirely abandoned its belief in the triumph of good and the destruction of evil. It is thus evident that throughout the whole history of Israel religion was in the most intimate connexion with morality.

Without seeking further to elaborate a point which seems almost self-evident, it may now be assumed that as a matter of historical fact there never has been any real antagonism between the religion and the morality of a people, but, on the contrary, the most intimate connexion. How, indeed, should it be otherwise, since every religion is an attempt to prevent the life of man from dissolving into a chaos of fragments by referring it to a principle which reduces it to order and coherence? There can be no morality without the belief in a life higher than sense and passion, and this belief must draw its support from faith in a divine principle which ensures victory to the higher life. We must not forget, however, that religion, like morality, is a process which can reach its goal only when the divine principle is so comprehensive that it explains the whole of life, and leaves no difficulty unsolved. Thus the religious and moral ideals of a people, though they sum up all that is best and noblest in its life, may fall far short of an ultimate explanation. That neither the Greek nor the Jewish ideal had reached a satisfactory conception of the true nature and relation of God, man, and the world, it will not be hard to show; and it is therefore obvious that a higher synthesis was imperatively demanded. But the important question, it will be said, is not whether Greece and Judea failed,— a proposition no one is likely to dispute,— but whether Christianity is not also another, even if it be a more splendid, failure. That this is the only really important question for us may be at once admitted, but it will hardly be denied that a clear conception of what the Christian ideal of life in its permanent essence is, and wherein its superiority to other ideals consists, is a necessary preparation for an intelligent estimate of its claim to be the ultimate ideal of life. To answer these questions thoroughly would involve a critical estimate of all the religions of the world. In the present essay, nothing so ambitious will be attempted; but perhaps a careful examination and comparison of the Greek, Jewish, and Christian ideals of life may be as convincing as a wider survey.

Before entering upon this task it may help to illustrate somewhat more fully the thesis of the present chapter, that religion and morality have always developed *pari passu*, if we glance at the different paths which the religious consciousness has followed among different peoples, and the goal which they have severally attained.

There seems reason to believe that all religions are either totemistic or have developed from totemism. We may, therefore, regard this form of religion as, if not the earliest, at least a very early form of religion. Traces of it are found even in those nations in which civilisation originated, and which reached a much higher ideal of life, such as the Chinese, the Indian, the Greek, and the Jewish; and indeed it is, as we have seen, the natural form in which the ideal of the family or the tribe is embodied, since that ideal is based entirely upon the tie of blood. We may thus regard totemism as the original matrix from which all other forms of religion were developed.

Totemism, however, gives way to a higher form of religion, whenever a people advances to anything like a settled form of society. This second stage of religion, among all the great nations of antiquity, except the Jewish, whose religious development is unique, consists in the worship of the divine as manifested in those universal powers of nature — the heavens, the sun, the winds, etc. — which exercise so large an influence upon the natural life of man, while yet they are altogether beyond the control of his will. Now it is easy to see how a people, who embodied their religious ideal in these great natural powers, should also have a higher moral ideal than races which never got beyond the stage of totemism. Early man found in his totem something higher than himself, but the divinity he ascribed to it was not so much in the object as in his own mind, or at least it was only in the object in the sense that nothing can exist which is not in some way a manifestation of the divine. But, when the divine is found in objects, which in force or splendour surpass the weak physical energy of man, the object selected is not altogether inadequate as a symbol of that spiritual power which man is feeling after; and as it is a universal object, it is not an inappropriate medium of the new ideal of a social unity embracing a number of tribes allied in blood. Thus the worship of the great powers of nature supplies a religious ideal which helps to unite all the members of allied tribes by the bond of a common faith.

From the worship of these natural powers the higher races advance to the stage of what is ordinarily called polytheism. The transition is effected by the tendency to personify those powers, and thus to bring them nearer to man. It is at this point that a highly significant divergence takes place, a divergence which determines the direction in which the subsequent development takes place. The Egyptian and Indian do indeed *personify* the gods, and thus for the time lift them out of the lower rank of mere powers of nature, but they do not *humanise* them. Hence their polytheism takes the form of what Mr. Max Müller has called henotheism. The tendency to unity, as well as multiplicity, is in operation from the very dawn of religion. Even races who have not advanced beyond the primitive stage of totemism always have a god who is regarded as higher than the other totems, and in nature-worship the heavens is naturally taken as the highest embodiment of the divine. The tendency to unification is therefore present from the first, but in the henotheistic phase of polytheism it assumes the peculiar form that each god becomes at the time of worship the only one who is present to the consciousness of the worshipper, and hence to him are attributed for the time being all the attributes which at other times are distributed among a number of gods. Now the importance of directing attention to this tendency to henotheism is that it explains why the Egyptian and Indian religions developed, not into monotheism, but into pantheism. The Greek religion, on the other hand, not only personified but humanised the gods, and the clearly cut types thus formed became a permanent possession of the race. Hence, when the Greek finally abandoned polytheism, his religion developed into monotheism, not into pantheism; and so long as he remained polytheistic the instinct for unity was satisfied by conceiving of Zeus as the Father and Ruler of the gods, or later as the representative of their united will. Now, whether polytheism assumes the henotheistic or the Greek form, it is obvious that it presents an ideal which serves to unite all the members of a nation by a common worship. Nor does it seem fanciful to say that polytheism is the natural form which the religious ideal assumes among nations which have been either formed into a single political unit by a combination of tribes allied in blood, or into a number of independent units united only by the bonds of a common descent and a common religion; in any case, it serves as the vehicle for the religious ideal of peoples who cannot conceive of a wider bond than that of the nation, or of the nation as other than a political unity based upon the natural tie of blood. Polytheism, therefore, tended to perpetuate absolute distinctions of caste, or of master and slave, and it naturally fostered a proud contempt for all who belonged to another nation, and therefore could not claim descent from the gods of their country. Here, therefore, we have another proof, if further proof were needed, of the close correspondence between religion and morality.

Polytheism, as has already been indicated, develops either into pantheism, or into monotheism. When it is of a henotheistic type, as in the case of the Egyptians and Indians, it naturally takes the former direction; the Greek religion, with its definitely characterised human types, as naturally follows the latter direction. Both the Egyptian and the Hindu are deficient in that poetic and artistic faculty, which is characteristic of the Greek, and hence they never succeed in imparting freedom and spirituality to their gods. With the rise of reflection the tendency to unity, which has already shown itself in their henotheism, carries them beyond the tendency to multiplicity, and as their gods have not been conceived as endowed with intelligence and will, they come to conceive of the divine as a purely abstract being, of which nothing can be said but that it *is*. To this religious ideal corresponds the ethical ideal. If the divine nature is absolutely without distinction, man can become divine only by the destruction of all that constitutes his separate individuality. Thus pantheism leads to the dissolution of all fixed moral distinctions, and therefore to the denial of any radical distinction between good and evil. "Whatever is, is right." It can therefore look with perfect calmness upon the wildest aberrations of passion, and it leads in men of a higher type to asceticism, only because it regards passion as a form of that universal illusion, or *Maya*, which supposes the finite to be real.

The Greek religion, as the product of a race of poets and artists, whose nature responded gladly to all the divine beauty and order of the world and of human life, could not thus pass into a joyless pantheism. Hence, under the influence of its poets and philosophers, it developed into a monotheism, in which the divine was conceived as a single spiritual Being, endowed with intelligence and will. It is significant that the Greeks only reached this stage, when their narrow civic state had already revealed its inadequacy, and when the bond of nationality, which had been hitherto preserved by loyalty to the national faith, had lost its power. Thus the wider conception of religion was reflected in the virtual dissolution of civic and national morality. It is time, however, to consider more carefully the strength and weakness of the Greek ideal of life. This will be done in the following chapter.

CHAPTER II

THE GREEK IDEAL

STARTING, like the other Indo-European peoples, from the worship of the great powers of nature, the Greeks developed a form of religion which is the highest type of polytheism. This religion was the embodiment of that love of beauty, truth, and freedom, which is distinctive of the Greek spirit. In the Homeric poems, the transition from the worship of nature has already been made. The gods are not only personified, but humanised. Turning his eyes to the expanse of heaven, the early Greek expressed his consciousness of the divine in the majestic form of Zeus, whose nod shook the whole heavens and the earth. The physical splendour of the sun became for him the radiant form of Apollo, shooting down gleaming arrows from his silver bow. Thus was gradually formed, not without the addition of new elements and even new gods, sometimes borrowed from Semitic sources but invariably transmuted into higher form, the pantheon of glorious shapes which filled the imagination of Homer. The divine nature is conceived as manifested in distinct types, each possessed of intelligence and will, and embodied in human forms, which exhibit the utmost perfection of physical beauty. These gracious forms only differ from man in the perfection of their spiritual and physical qualities, and in their freedom from decay and death. Thus the Greek expresses in his religion his ideal of perfect manhood as the complete harmony of soul and body. Were it possible to secure and retain for ever physical, intellectual, and moral beauty, the ideal of the early Greek would be realised. That ideal, however, was one which did not separate the good of the individual from the good of society. Achilles is distinguished, not merely by splendid physical beauty, powers, and eloquence, but by his burning indignation against wrong: and, when he carries his resentment against Agamemnon to an extreme which threatens the destruction of the whole Greek host, he is punished by an untimely death. So Zeus is the impersonation of a wise and just ruler, Apollo the divine type of the poetic and religious mind, Athena the ideal of valour directed and kept in check by wise self-restraint. The Greek gods are thus the expression of the Greek ideal of a society in which the highest natural qualities are valued as a means to the realisation of a free community. The Homeric king is not a despot, but the guardian of the sacred customs on which the rights of his subjects are based. He does nothing without consulting his council of elders, and the public assembly consists of the whole body of citizens. The world of the gods is an idealised counterpart of the heroic form of society; and, in fact, the early Greek could only conceive of the divine as a community of gods, living in each other's society, and sympathising with the fortunes of men.

The Homeric gods are thus the embodiment of that free and joyous existence which was the ideal of life of the early Greek. The Greek religion is essentially a religion of this world; for, though the Greek believed in a shadowy realm of the dead, his heart was set upon the beauty, the joy, the sunlight of this world, and he looked forward to the future life, without dread, indeed, but with a melancholy resignation. With his intrepid intellect he had a clear and sober apprehension of the shortness of life and the limitations of humanity, but he had not yet lost the fresh exuberance of the youth of the world; and in devotion to his country and faith in divine justice, he found all that was needed to satisfy his highest desires. Entirely free from a slavish dread of the gods, he came into their presence with joyous confidence. He did not forget that his destiny lay on the knees of the gods, but, having perfect faith in their justice, he did not prostrate himself before them with the abject submission of the Asiatic.

The charm of this conception of life has never failed to exercise a peculiar fascination, and indeed it contains elements which must be embodied in the modern ideal, though these must be transmuted into a higher form. Its fundamental defect is that it can be approximately realised only by those who possess exceptional gifts of nature and fortune, and that it conceives of the highest life as simply the expansion of the natural life. The Greek was destitute of that profound consciousness of the Infinite which was characteristic of the Jewish religion, and therefore of the wide interval between man as he is and as he ought to be. No doubt in his deepest nature man is identical with God, but his deepest nature reveals itself only when he turns against his immediate self. Of this truth the Greek had no proper apprehension, and therefore he never got beyond the ideal of a perfect natural life, in which the spiritual and natural were in harmony with each other, and of a State in which the individual citizen found his complete satisfaction in devotion to the common weal. That this limited ideal could not be permanently satisfactory is shown by the gradual emergence of a deeper conception of life, which as time went on came more and more into the foreground, until it finally led, in the poets and philosophers, to a complete transformation of the earlier belief.

Though the Greek religion is the highest form of polytheism, it has, like all polytheistic religions, the fundamental defect of having no adequate idea of the unity and spirituality of the divine nature. This defect is, in the Greek form of polytheism, made all the more prominent by the individuality ascribed to the gods. The gods, as embodied in sensible human form, are limited in space and time, and hence their relation to man is inadequately conceived. There can be no proper comprehension of the unity and spirituality of the divine nature, so long as the divine is conceived as merely the perfection of the natural. Beings who are regarded as limited in space and time cannot be the source of all reality, and their relation to man can only be external. Hence the Greek gods themselves were conceived as having come into existence at a definite time, and their action upon men was represented as their actual sensible appearance to their favourites. Athena presents herself in human shape to Achilles, and persuades him to abandon his purpose of slaying Agamemnon; Aphrodite hides Paris in a cloud when he flees from the spear of Menelaus. Thus the life of man is represented as directly interfered with by the gods, so that man seems to be merely a puppet in their hands. This defect is inseparable from the pictorial form of the religion, which necessarily represents the spiritual as on the same plane with the natural.

Even in Homer, however, there are elements which show that the Greek religion must ultimately accomplish its own euthanasia. There was in it from the first a latent contradiction which could not fail to manifest itself openly at a later time. The very concreteness and humanity of the gods was at variance with the instinct for unity, which could neither be suppressed nor reconciled with the polytheistic basis of the traditional faith. To a certain extent that instinct was satisfied by the conception of Zeus as the "Father of gods and men," whose authority, though it is not absolute, is higher than that of the other gods. But this conception could only be temporarily satisfactory; and, indeed, even in Homer, there is already indicated a deeper sort of unity, which is inconsistent with this mere unity of the pictorial imagination. For Homer, like his successors, was strongly impressed with the belief that the life of man is subject to divine control, and that his destiny is determined in accordance with absolute principles of justice. Paris violates the sacred bond which united host and guest, and punishment falls upon himself and all his kindred. The Trojans break the oath to which they had solemnly sworn, and draw down upon themselves the punishment which they deserved. There was thus an absolute faith in the righteous judgments of the gods. Such a faith could not be reconciled with the caprice, partiality, and lawlessness, which were ascribed to the gods in their individual character. For they are represented as not only violating accepted moral laws, but as at variance with one another, and guilty of gross favouritism. This unreconciled antagonism was partly due to the survival of earlier and less elevated ideas of the divine nature, to which custom and tradition lent an adventitious sanctity, but it was also inseparable from the anthropomorphism of the Greek religion. The conflict of competing ideas is especially apparent in the conception of Zeus, whose character as an individual is widely different from what has been called his official character as the exponent of the common will of the gods. Sometimes Homer speaks of Zeus as rewarding or punishing men; sometimes this power is vested in the gods as a whole. In the *Iliad* Zeus is called the guardian of oaths, while yet Agamemnon speaks of the sufferings inflicted by "the gods" upon those who swear falsely. In the *Odyssey* there are even passages in which an abrupt transition is made from the gods to Zeus, as when Telemachus invokes the gods, "If perchance Zeus will punish the wickedness of the suitors (I. 378)." This tendency to conceive of Zeus as the sole administrator of justice, which is manifest even in the Homeric poems, becomes more and more pronounced, so that in the period between Homer and the Persian wars, it is almost invariably Zeus who is spoken of as the guardian of moral order. Thus, without any explicit rejection of polytheism, there was a continual tendency to transcend it. Isocrates, who is the spokesman, not of philosophers like Anaxagoras, but of the educated common sense of his time, explains the poetic representation of Zeus as king of the gods by the natural tendency to figure the divine government after the fashion of an earthly state. Besides this explicit criticism of the popular faith, the striving after a higher idea of the divine is shown in the reverential feeling which led the worshipper, in calling upon one of the gods to add, "or by whatever name thou mayst desire to be called." But nothing shows more clearly the tendency to go beyond the earlier mode of thought than the indefinite terms by which the divine power is designated by the prose writers. They still, no doubt, speak of "the gods," but they usually employ such expressions as "the divine," "the god," "the dæmonic," when they have to speak of the moral government of the world.

There is thus in the development of Greek thought a clearly marked tendency to unity, manifesting itself, on the one hand, in the conception of Zeus as the exponent of the common will of the gods; and, on the other hand, in the conception of "something divine," which was not definitely embodied in the gods of the popular faith. It has been held that the Greek conception of a "fate," to which the gods as well as men are subject, indicates a certain pantheistic tendency in the Greek mind, which was only kept in check by the opposite tendency to conceive of the divine as personal. This view seems to imply that every attempt to transcend particularism and anthropomorphism indicates a movement towards pantheism. It seems more natural to say that the movement beyond polytheism may be either towards pantheism or monotheism, and that the special direction which the movement takes will be determined by the peculiar form of the polytheism which forms the starting-point. In the Greek mind, which humanised the gods, the reaction against particularism was naturally towards monotheism. The idea of "fate" was therefore conceived, not as a mere external necessity, but as a rational law, and the gods were regarded as subject to it only in the sense that even the divine nature was not beyond law.

The more firmly the conception of a moral government of the world was grasped, the clearer was the apprehension of the apparent exceptions to it. In Homer and Hesiod, faith in divine justice assumes the simple form of a belief that the pious man is directly rewarded by a happy and fortunate life. In the *Odyssey* Ulysses says, that when a king is pious and just, the land is fruitful and the people prosperous. Hesiod declares that on the just man, who keeps his oath, Zeus bestows more renown and a fairer posterity than on the unjust. It was a popular belief that impiety never fails to be punished by blindness, madness, or death. To the objection that the innocent were sometimes unfortunate, it was answered that they were involved in the misfortunes of the wicked. The similar difficulty that the wicked are often prosperous was met by saying that divine justice, though it may be delayed, always overtakes them in the end. The same idea is expressed in the well-known saying of an unknown poet, that "the mills of the gods grind slow but very small." A further modification of the idea of divine retribution was that, though the wicked man may himself escape, misfortune is sure to fall upon his posterity. We also find among the Greeks a growing scepticism of the reality of divine justice, but the best minds surmounted this scepticism by a deeper view of the relation between the divine and human,—a view which was most fully developed by Æschylus and Sophocles. In these poets, in fact, the current religious and moral ideas were so deepened as to result in an ethical monotheism, though they never consciously surrendered the polytheism of the popular faith.

Æschylus, the poet of the men who fought at Marathon and Salamis, has unbounded faith in the gods of his country. At the same time his plastic imagination works freely on the mass of legendary material which he found ready to his hand, and into the old bottles he pours the new wine of a higher conception of the divine nature and the destiny of man. This transforming process is exhibited in his reconstruction of the myth of Prometheus. Zeus, the representative of intelligence and order, when he has dethroned Chronos, finds on the earth the miserable race of men. Their champion, the Titan Prometheus, steals "the flashing fire, mother of all arts," and conveys it to men in a hollow reed. For his insolence and deceit he must undergo proportional punishment, until he has repented and submitted to the sovereign will of Zeus. Suffering but intensifies his proud and rebellious spirit, and it is only after long ages of punishment, and through the influence of Heracles, the godlike man, whose life has been spent in toil for others, that he is at last induced to give up his purpose of revenge. There seems little doubt that here, as elsewhere, Æschylus seeks to show that the world is governed with absolute justice, and that the true lesson of life is to submit to the divine will. When man sets up his own rebellious will against the Ruler of the universe, he must expect divine punishment. The triple Fates and the mindful Erinyes jealously guard the sanctity of the primal ties. The doom of Troy is the divine punishment for violated hospitality. Agamemnon perishes because his hands are stained with his daughter's blood. Æschylus explicitly rejects the old doctrine of the envy of the gods: it is sinful rebellion against the divine law which brings punishment in its train. The sins of the fathers are no doubt visited upon the children, but the curse never falls upon those whose hands are pure. The house of Atreus seems the prey of a malign, inevitable fate, but only because in each new representative there is a frenzy of wickedness, an infatuate hardening of the heart. When, therefore, a pure scion of this accursed stock appears, the curse is removed: he suffers indeed, but his end is peace; and at last he returns in honour to reign over the house which he has cleansed. Thus the Erinyes become the Eumenides: the stern law of justice turns at last a gracious face to those who fear and honour the gods.

But, while Æschylus conceives of Zeus as the divine representative of the whole order of society, the divine law is still conceived by him as an external law to which man must submit. Sophocles, on the other hand, while he endorses the conception of a divine law of justice, seeks to show that this law operates in man as the law of his own reason. Œdipus unwittingly violates the sacred bond of the family, and punishment inevitably follows; but his punishment is also the recoil upon himself of his defiant self-assertion, and therefore, when he recognises that his suffering was not unmerited, he is at last reconciled to the divine will and comes to harmony with himself. Yet even in Sophocles the limitation of the Greek ideal of life is manifest; for, though he views suffering as a means of purification from self-assertion and overweening pride, he does not reach the conception that in self-sacrifice the true nature of man is revealed; the highest point to which he attains is the conception that man can reach happiness only by voluntary submission to the divine will, which is also the law of his own reason. It is only in Euripides that we find something like an anticipation of the Christian idea that self-realisation is attained through self-sacrifice. In Euripides, however, this result is reached by a surrender of his faith in the divine justice. Man, he seems to say, is capable of heroic self-sacrifice at the prompting of natural affection, but this is the law of human nature, not of the divine nature. Thus in him morality is divorced from religion, and therefore there is over all his work the sadness which inevitably follows from a sceptical distrust of the existence of any objective principle of goodness. This division of religion and morality could not be final, and hence the attempts of Plato and Aristotle to restore the broken harmony by a higher conception of the divine nature.

Though the transformation of the Greek religion by the great poets of Greece was a continuous movement towards a more spiritual view of the divine nature, it did not involve an explicit breach with polytheism, except in the case of Euripides. Æschylus and

Sophocles, though they virtually affirm the unity and spirituality of the divine will, are not in conscious antagonism to the popular faith. Such an antagonism was, however, inevitable, so soon as philosophical reflection arose, and proceeded to ask how far mythology could be accepted as historical truth. The question could not be raised without producing a temporary scepticism. The first philosophers were therefore almost entirely negative in their attitude towards the traditional faith.* It was only with Socrates and his followers that a perception of the rational element implied in mythology was apprehended. Hence, while Plato is severe in his condemnation of the unworthy representations of the divine nature in Homer and Hesiod, he recognises that the imaginative form which that faith assumed was a necessary stage in the education of the race and of the individual. Poetry is a "lie," no doubt, but it is a "noble lie." Plato is here seeking to separate the form from the

* "Whether there are gods or not I cannot tell," said Protagoras; "life is too short for such obscure problems."

matter, the spirit from the earthly tabernacle in which it is enclosed. The divine, as he contends, is not immoral, malicious, or deceitful. What he is really seeking to show is that the divine nature transcends the sensible, and is the ultimate source of all truth, beauty, and goodness. Plato does not, in the first instance, reject the pictorial representations of the popular imagination, which he no doubt regarded as inseparable from the poetic garb endeared to the Greek heart by the hallowing associations of ages; but he insists that the gods must not be portrayed as violating the sanctities of moral law, as inflicting evil upon man from envy, or as appearing in lower forms. The gods are absolutely good, truthful, and beautiful, and therefore are eternally and unchangeably the same. It is obvious, however, that Plato does not at bottom believe that the divine nature can be represented in sensible form at all, and hence we cannot be surprised that, with his imperfect theory of art as an "imitation" of sensible reality, the more he reflects upon the distorting influence of all imaginative representations of the divine nature, the more dissatisfied he becomes, until at last he concludes, though with great reluctance, that there is no place for the poet in that ideal city of which he dreamed such beautiful, philosophical dreams. The preparation for this extreme view is already made in the contention that poetry is a "lie," even if it is a "noble lie," and in the denial that evil can in any sense proceed from God, or that the divine can ever be manifested except in its own absolutely perfect form. For the representation of what is false, though it may be necessary as an educational device, has no ultimate justification; the Manichean separation of evil from the divine is at the same time the exclusion of God from the actual world; and the only perfect form of the divine must be the supersensible. Thus, by the natural development of Greek thought, Plato is at last led to maintain a spiritual monotheism, resembling in its main features the conception of God, which by an independent path was reached by the Hebrew people in the later stages of their history. In his revolt from the pictorial representations of the divine, he is led to conceive of God as dwelling in a transcendent region beyond the actual world, and this, though a necessary step in the evolution of the religious consciousness, is not the last word of religion. The Infinite cannot be severed from the finite, God from man, without becoming itself finite, unless we are prepared to regard the finite as pure illusion. Nor does Aristotle, though he protests against the Platonic separation of the real and the ideal, succeed in avoiding the rock on which Plato's philosophy of religion makes shipwreck; for he too conceives of God as a purely contemplative being, alone with Himself, and self-sufficient in His isolation, who acts upon the world only as the sculptor hews and shapes the block of marble, which can never be quite divested of its material grossness.

If this is at all a fair account of the theology of Plato and Aristotle, we must admit that their solutions are not final. The negative movement by which the creations of art and the products of the religious consciousness in its imaginative form have been rejected, and the first unquestioning faith in the outward manifestation of reason in nature and human life "sicklied o'er with the pale cast of thought," is only imperfectly supplemented by a positive movement in which the real is virtually declared to lie beyond the actual. For, so long as the world of our experience is regarded as containing an irrational element, the human spirit must either fall back baffled upon the phenomenal, or seek to fly beyond the "flaming walls of the world" by some other organ than reason. It is, therefore, not surprising that Plato and Aristotle were succeeded, on the one hand by the individualistic philosophies of the Stoics, Epicureans, and Sceptics, and on the other hand by the Neo-platonists and Gnostics, who in despair of reason took refuge in a supposed "immediate intuition" or "ecstasy."

CHAPTER III

THE JEWISH IDEAL

THE religion of Greece, as we have seen, developed from a humanistic polytheism, through the influence of its great poets and philosophers, into monotheism. Even in its polytheistic stage there was a marked tendency towards unity, but this tendency was not realised until Plato affirmed the unity and spirituality of the divine nature. The religion of Israel reached the same point by a more direct path. There seems to be clear evidence that Israel had passed from a primitive totemism to the worship of great powers of nature before the captivity in Egypt. Evidence of the former stage is to be found in the household gods or teraphim, and of the latter in the early conception of Jehovah as the God of the tempest, who had His seat on Mount Sinai. What is unique in the development of the religion of Israel is that it passed without a break from the worship of nature, to the worship of Jehovah, without going through the intermediate stage of polytheism. This peculiarity arose from the whole character and history of the people. Unlike the Greeks, the people of Israel had no artistic faculty, and what moved them in nature was not the beauty of the world, but the tremendous energy manifested in its more terrible aspects. The divine power they saw manifested in the thunder, and in the tempest which broke on the mountains of Sinai and rolled across the desert. This great and terrible Lord was, from the time of their deliverance from servitude in Egypt under their great leader Moses, the common object of worship of all the tribes. Thus even before their political union, the belief in Jehovah was the bond which kept them united as a people, and after the loss of their national independence it kept them separate and distinct from all other nations. It is true that, after their settlement in Canaan, there was a continual struggle between those who worshipped only Jehovah and those who saw no harm in combining His worship with that of other gods; but the great name of Jehovah never failed to reunite all the tribes in their struggle for independence, and so to prevent them from being merged in the surrounding tide of Canaanite life. And when the monarchy was founded, and the religion of Jehovah became the national religion, the intense consciousness of their great past and the anticipation of a still greater future made it impossible that their faith in Jehovah should ever be completely lost.

Up to the time of the great prophets, Jehovah was conceived only as the greatest of all gods, the God of Israel, who went before them in battle and led them to victory, and who was pledged to aid His people in their time of need. Thus the religious faith of Israel was bound up with a belief in the permanence of its nationality. It was the work of the great prophets to free the conception of Jehovah from its exclusively national character. In effecting this change, they were but developing what was implicit in the conception from the first. He who was at first conceived to be manifested in the great and terrible aspects of nature came to be regarded as raised entirely above nature, and the God of battles was transformed into the God of holiness. Hence, though Jehovah is still conceived as standing in a more intimate relation to Israel than to other nations, it is maintained that this relation can continue only if Israel is pre-eminent in righteousness. "You only have I known of all the families of the earth, therefore I will punish you for all your iniquities." Israel must no longer regard herself as secure of the divine favour, irrespective of her conduct: if she continues to dishonour Jehovah, her nationality will be destroyed. This is the idea which Isaiah insists upon with such fervour and power. Even when the kingdoms of Judah and Israel were in the full tide of prosperity, the prophet discovered in them the seeds of decay. The upper class was materialised, and the lower class full of superstition and practical unbelief. The result was inevitable: their cities will be wasted and the land left desolate, though, as the prophet believes, there will always be a remnant to form the nucleus of a new and regenerate nation. Jehovah will employ the great heathen powers as an instrument for the punishment of Israel. A people who fail in the practice of justice and mercy cannot hope for the favour of a righteous and holy God.

It is obvious that in this new conception the old idea of Jehovah as the God only of Israel has been virtually transcended. Accordingly the prophets deny that there is any God but Jehovah, and, therefore, declare that He has relations to other nations as well as to Israel. He governs the world, not in the interests of one nation only, but in the interests of righteousness. He is the Creator of all things, and the Ruler of the universe, though He has specially revealed Himself to Israel.

In the later prophets a further advance is made. Jehovah is not only the God of nations, but He is directly related to the individual soul. This advance followed as a natural consequence of the conception of God as a God of righteousness. A God who is beyond nature, and is essentially spiritual, cannot be permanently conceived as related only to the nation. Holiness depends upon the inner state of the soul, and therefore the relation of man to God is a personal one. Hence Jeremiah and Ezekiel assert personal responsibility. "Every one shall die for his own iniquity," says Jeremiah; and Ezekiel declares that "the soul that sinneth, it shall die."

With the conception of God as absolutely holy, and the demand for perfect purity of heart and conduct, there arose the consciousness of the opposition between the finite and the infinite, the actual and the ideal. Thus the religion of Israel, unlike the Greek, is a religion of prophecy. The prophet, maintaining that man was originally made "a little lower than God," and contrasting with this perfect relation his present sinfulness, looks forward to a time when the unity with God which has been lost shall be restored.

The higher conception of religion and morality taught by the prophets was not immediately accepted by the people, though the successive reforms narrated in the histories show that it had commended itself to the best minds. It was only with the exile that the people obtained a firm grasp of the idea that they were the custodians of the one true religion. This conviction finds its most perfect expression in the second Isaiah, who declares that the peculiar mission of Israel is to make known the true God to the heathen. There will always be a faithful "remnant" entirely devoted to the service of Jehovah, who, even if they suffer for the sins of others, will be the means of leading many to righteousness.

With the cessation of the fresh spring of prophetic utterance, the Jewish conception of God tended to become more and more abstract. The way was prepared for this change by the formation, under Ezra and Nehemiah, of a sort of theocratic commonwealth, a compact and homogeneous little state, devoted mainly to the worship of Jehovah. With the establishment of this community, the separation of Israel from the rest of the world, and the subsequent worship of the letter of scripture, were inevitable. Jerusalem became the universally acknowledged centre of the religion and worship of Jehovah, to which from time to time Israelites from all parts of the earth flocked to offer sacrifice in the temple. Though this centralisation of sacrificial worship was a bond of union to the despised race, it was not effective as a national bond, while on the other hand it was hostile to the wider bond of humanity. Indirectly, the centralisation of worship in Jerusalem gave rise to the institution of the synagogue. This change had important consequences. Religion became no longer merely national, but individual. The most beautiful flower of this personal religion was its sacred lyrical poetry. Many of the psalms, most of which are admitted to belong to the centuries after the exile, express the pure and pious feeling called forth by the reading of the Law and the prophets in the synagogue. There was, however, another consequence of the change. The importance of the sacerdotal cultus in Jerusalem receded into the background. The Levite became of less consequence than the Rabbi skilled in the Law. Thus the Law came to be the centre of all the thoughts of the pious Israelite. The whole education of the people, in the family, the school, and the synagogue, was intended to make them a "people of the law." No longer did Jehovah reveal His will through the direct inspiration of a prophet. A final revelation of Himself had been given in the Law, and the sole duty of His people was to find out by a careful examination of the words of Scripture what had been revealed once for all. Shut out from the direct consciousness of God, the conception of His nature became more and more abstract. He was "the Holy One," the "Absolute," raised to an infinite distance above the world and man, even to name whom was profane. Religion thus came to be regarded, not as the communion of man with God, but as the right relation of man before God. The Law took the place formerly occupied by God. It is identified with the eternal wisdom, which arose from the unknown depths of the divine nature; it is the image or daughter of God, which was before the creation of the world, and in the contemplation of which the divine life is passed. As expressing the whole nature of God, the Law is the ultimate revelation, valid for all time and even for eternity; it is the true food of the soul, the tree of life, the source of all knowledge. The essence of religion, therefore, consists in love of the Law, as exhibited in its study and in observance of its precepts. Thus the Law at once unites Israel to Jehovah, and separates her from the whole heathen world, which by its rejection of the Law at Sinai adopted a hostile attitude toward Jehovah.

As conformity to the Law was the standard and source of all righteousness, God was bound by the terms of the covenant entered into with Israel to recompense the pious Israelite in proportion to his observance of its precepts. As this proportion was not always observed, it was held that at some future time the balance would be restored.

The whole religious life thus revolved around these two poles, — conformity to the Law and the hope of future reward. Under such a purely external conception, religion and morality were emptied of life. For that free and spontaneous devotion to goodness which is of the very essence of the spiritual life, was substituted the mechanical observance of rules imposed by external authority. The Law was to be obeyed, not because it expressed the true nature of man, but because it had been ordained by Him who had power to reward and punish. As its various precepts were not seen to flow from any principle, the moral life was conceived to consist in strict obedience to every detail of the Law. Where all was equally imposed by God, every requirement of the Law had the same absolute claim to obedience. Thus there was, in St. Paul's phrase, "a zeal for God, but not according to knowledge." To the conscientious Israelite, life was made an intolerable burden, while the rigid adherent of the Law could hardly escape from a proud and boastful self-righteousness.

The logical consequences of this legalistic

religion and morality are most clearly seen in the life and theory of the Pharisees, who carried out to its extreme the spirit which rules the whole post-exilic period. It has sometimes been said that the Pharisees were the patriotic party, as contrasted with the Sadducees, who were always ready to sacrifice their country and even the national religion from motives of worldly prudence. It would seem, however, that the main spring of action in the Pharisees was not love of country, but love of the Law. And by the Law they meant, not so much the written as the "oral" law, which had been gradually formed by the labours of the scribes. "The Pharisees," says Josephus, "have imposed upon the people many laws taken from the tradition of the fathers, which are not written in the Law of Moses." Such an extension of the Law was inevitable. A law accepted upon authority necessarily gives rise to casuistry, the moment an attempt is made to make it a complete guide of life; and the precedents thus established naturally come to be regarded as an unfolding of what is already contained in the law. What distinguished the Pharisees was their claim to peculiar strictness in the interpretation and observance of the Law, or rather of the "traditions of the fathers," and especially of the laws relating to cleanness and uncleanness. They regarded themselves as the true Israel, in distinction not only from the heathen, but from the less scrupulous of their own countrymen. That excessive zeal for the letter of the Law was their ruling motive seems to be proved by their attitude to successive dynasties. During the Maccabean conflict, they adopted the popular cause; but when the insurrection proved successful, and the Asmoneans showed indifference to the Law, the Pharisees turned against them. Their zeal for the Law won the people to their side, and henceforth they completely ruled the public life. Even the direction of public worship was in the hands of the Pharisees, though the priestly Sadducees were nominally the head of the Sanhedrim. The Sadducees were the wealthy, aristocratic party, and therefore belonged mainly to the priesthood, which, as far back as the Persian period, governed the Jewish state and formed its nobility. They differed from the Pharisees in acknowledging only the Pentateuch and the prophets as binding, to the exclusion of the whole mass of legal decisions which had been established by the Pharisaic scribes. The Sadducees held fast by the older faith, mainly because they were averse to the bigotry and exclusiveness of the Pharisees. As a matter of fact their position as men of affairs, and their contact with foreign culture, had made them comparatively indifferent to the religion of their fathers.

The Messianic hopes of the Pharisees were the natural complement of their legalism. They believed that, in terms of the covenant made at Sinai, God was bound to reward those who obeyed the Law, and therefore that the political and individual evils to which the saints were subjected could only be temporary. They therefore looked forward to a time when the whole world would be united under the sceptre of Israel into a universal monarchy, over which the Messiah should be ruler and judge. In this glorious era, the pious individual would also be rewarded. The general belief was in a "resurrection of the just," though some also expected a general resurrection, when the wicked should be punished and the righteous rewarded. The reign of the saints was to be ushered in by the direct intervention of God, when the rule of Satan and his angels should give place to the rule of God and His anointed. The Messiah, the King of Israel, chosen by God from all eternity, should come down from heaven, where He was already in communion with God, and establish upon earth the reign of righteousness and peace. While this was the form which the Messianic hope assumed in the minds of the scribes and Pharisees, there were not wanting men of a finer type, in whose minds it was accompanied by the expectation of the triumph of good over evil, and of the deliverance of man from the evil of his own heart. A consideration of the attitude of Jesus toward the Law and the Messianic hopes of his time will help to bring out the distinctive features of the Christian, as distinguished from the Jewish, ideal of life.

CHAPTER IV

THE CHRISTIAN IDEAL

THE first step toward the overthrow of the whole set of legalistic ideas, characteristic of later Judaism, was taken by John the Baptist. It is true that the Baptist did not break with the legal piety of his time, but his watchword, " Repent, for the kingdom of heaven is at hand," was in essence a denial of the principle upon which legalism rested. For, according to that principle, the delay of the kingdom of heaven was not due to the unrighteousness of Israel, but to the inscrutable designs of providence, which permitted Satan with his host of angels to afflict the saints and deprive them of the reward to which their diligent observance of the Law entitled them. The reign of the saints could only come with the miraculous advent of the Messiah. The Baptist, on the other hand, found the explanation of the delay in the manifestation of the kingdom of heaven in the sinfulness of men, not in the inscrutable designs of God. Hence he called for repentance, and, by demanding from every one a confession of sin, he virtually denied that the Pharisees were justified in regarding themselves as righteous. The evils from which men suffered were not due to the malevolence of evil spirits, but to their own corrupt hearts. No doubt the blessings of the kingdom of heaven could only come from above, but only those need hope to participate in them who were conscious of the evil of their own hearts, and sought the righteousness of God. The kingdom of heaven was at hand, and the necessary preparation for it was a "change of mind."

The effect of this message upon the Pharisees could only be to arouse their indignation and rancour; for, in demanding from all a confession of sin and a change of heart, the Baptist struck a powerful blow at their self-righteousness and spiritual pride; and, in virtually affirming that righteousness did not consist in the scrupulous observance of the Law, he denied the very foundation upon which they based their expectation of future reward. To those finer spirits, on the other hand, who were painfully conscious of their own weakness and sinfulness, the preaching of the Baptist came as a welcome solution of their spiritual perplexities, and helped to restore their faith in the justice of God.

Among those who at once discerned the significance of the Baptist's summons to repentance was Jesus, who submitted to baptism, as a sign of his belief in the fundamental truth of John's doctrine, and, indeed, in the beginning of his ministry, adopted as his own the watchword, "Repent, for the kingdom of heaven is at hand." But, while Jesus thus endorsed the new way of righteousness, it soon became evident that he gave to it another and a deeper meaning. In the Beatitudes this new point of view is already indicated. Repentance is by the Baptist conceived as the moral preparation for a deliverance from evil which is still future;

by Jesus it is regarded as consisting in a personal consciousness of the infinite love of God. Thus the moral revolution is inseparable from the religious. The kingdom of heaven is already present in the souls of those who have an absolute faith in the goodness of God, a faith which finds expression in unselfish devotion to their fellow-men, and which rejoices in revilings and persecutions as the process through which goodness gradually overcomes evil.

The ideal of life which is indicated in the Beatitudes was an entire reversal of the current conception, especially as it had been formulated in the teaching of the scribes and Pharisees. Even the method of exposition was new; for, whereas the accepted teachers in all cases sought to deduce conclusions from the letter of scripture, by a laborious and ingenious system of exegesis, Jesus threw out his ideas in the form of aphorisms, which shone by their own light. And if his method was thus free and unconventional, how much more revolutionary seemed to be the substance of his teaching!

Ignoring the authority of the Law and the prophets, he seemed to assert an independent basis for the new truth which he proclaimed, and, in making righteousness consist entirely in a spiritual regeneration, he apparently despised the whole body of truth which had been revealed by God himself to Moses and the prophets. It was, therefore, charged against him that, in abrogating the Law, he was destroying the very foundation of religion and morality. The objection is one which never fails to be made when the principle of external authority is attacked. When Socrates sought to trace back the customary religious and moral ideas of his time to their principle, he was accused of denying the gods of his country, and corrupting the minds of the youth; and the similar charge was brought against St. Paul, that in destroying the authority of the Law, he was virtually the advocate of licentiousness and impiety. The answer of Jesus was, that so far from abrogating the Mosaic law he "fulfilled" it; *i.e.* brought to light the principle which gave it its binding force. The Law, as he contends, is of eternal obligation, and cannot be abolished so long as heaven and earth endure. "Think not that I came to destroy the law and the prophets; I came not to destroy but to fulfil." The new way of life does not abolish the Law, but shows that it cannot be abolished. On the other hand, the old way of basing it upon external authority and custom destroys its very foundation. The source of all morality is to be found, not in the external act, but in the inner spirit from which the act proceeds, and when this is once seen it becomes evident that the legalism of the scribes and Pharisees is antagonistic to any genuine morality.

The Law which is thus declared to be eternal and indestructible is the Law in its moral, as distinguished from its ceremonial, part. It is the Law as interpreted from the point of view of the prophets. This distinction of the ethical from the ceremonial part of the Law is of itself an important advance. It is a distinction which could have no meaning for the scribes and Pharisees, who had no criterion by which to separate between what

F

was based upon the unchanging nature of man and what held good only under special circumstances and at a given stage in the development of humanity. For, as we have seen, a law which is accepted purely upon authority, is all equally binding. But this is not all; for not only does Jesus distinguish the ethical from the ceremonial part of the Law, but he goes back beyond the traditional morality of his day to the fundamental moral ideas expressed in the Law and the prophets, and disengages the principle upon which they rest. Thus he is enabled to grasp the Law in its purity and universality, and to contrast it with the unspiritual interpretations of the scribes.

Take, *e.g.* the command: " Thou shalt not kill." The scribes, in accordance with their usual conception of morality as a system of external rewards and punishments, add the gloss: " Whosoever shall kill, shall be in danger of the judgment." The sanction of the Law is thus made to consist, not in the sacredness of human life, but in the fear of punishment here or hereafter.

The principle upon which the Law is based is therefore destroyed. The appeal is to a purely selfish motive, and with that appeal the whole moral aspect of the Law disappears. Jesus, on the other hand, insists that the command rests upon the purely moral principle of love, and that the Law is violated in its essence, not merely in this extreme expression of hatred, but in hatred in all its forms, or rather in that evil disposition which is the source of all hatred. The outward act has no moral meaning in itself; murder is not the mere taking away of life, but the taking away of life from hatred to one's fellow-man; and therefore anger, want of sympathy, and contempt, as springing from the same corrupt source, the unloving heart, are worthy of the most extreme punishment, the "hell of fire." Thus the Law is seen to exclude the whole range of malevolent passions and even the faintest taint of hatred. Jesus was therefore justified in saying that the righteousness of his followers must "exceed the righteousness of the scribes and Pharisees," and "exceed" it not merely in degree, but in kind. The distinction, in fact, is infinite. The scribes, in conceiving morality to consist solely in conformity to an external rule, irrespective of the motive from which the act proceeded, virtually did away with the whole principle of morality; and, by their reduction of morality to a system of external rewards and punishments, they violated the very essence of morality, which rests upon the universal principle of brotherly love. To this it is added that morality is the prerequisite of all true worship: no genuine religious act can be performed by the man who nourishes in his heart a grudge against his neighbour. Lastly, Jesus traces back the ethical principle of love to one's neighbour to a fundamental identity in the nature of God and man: hatred brings upon the man who nourishes it its own punishment, just because he is violating what is his own real self; and hence, though he may escape external punishment, he cannot possibly escape the most terrible of all punishments,—that which consists in the loss of the blessedness which springs from the consciousness of unity with God.

The same principle is applied to other moral laws; in all cases Jesus traces back the command to its source in the nature of man as identical in nature with God. At the close of his treatment of this theme he expands the principle of morality so as to embrace all men, and he elevates it into infinity. The Law had said: "Thou shalt not hate thy brother in thine heart, thou shalt not be angry with the children of thy people, thou shalt love thy neighbour as thyself (Lev. xix. 17, 18)." From this precept came the characteristic Pharisaic deduction: "Thou shalt be angry with the stranger, thou shalt hate thine enemies." Thus national hatred was not only condoned, but was actually made a principle of action, and surrounded with all the sanctity and solemnity of a divine command. Now even Plato reached the conception that "it was better to suffer than to do injustice." Jesus goes altogether beyond this negative attitude. "Love your enemies, and pray for them that persecute you." This is, indeed, a "new commandment." It is the very core of Christian ethics — that which gives it its superiority, and makes it inconceivable that its principle can ever be transcended. Moreover, this supreme ethical principle is immediately connected with the distinctively Christian idea of God, as the "Father" of men, whose love has absolutely no limits. As a symbol of this all-embracing love, he "maketh his sun to rise on the evil and the good, and sendeth his rain on the just and the unjust." "Therefore," concludes Jesus, "Ye shall be perfect as your heavenly Father is perfect"; *i.e.* man, finite and sinful as he is, is yet capable of living a divine life, of repeating on an infinitesimal scale the large all-embracing charity of his heavenly "Father."

Jesus has thus vindicated the "Law" as an expression of the fundamental moral ideas which constitute the soul of society. It is evident, however, that in tracing back those ideas to their source, he has raised them to a plane which was never dreamt of before; in other words, he has virtually abolished the conception of man and God upon which the Jewish religion rested. At the same time the new way of life is not an absolute change, but a development. The moral laws won for humanity by the toil and suffering of the Jewish people were not lost, though they underwent expansion and specification by the appreciation of the principle of universal brotherhood. Of this double relation Jesus was perfectly conscious. Hence, while on the one hand he affirms the eternal obligation of the Law, he asserts with equal decision that the new principle which he brought to light separates the new world from the old as by an impassable barrier. "From the days of John the Baptist until now the kingdom of heaven suffereth violence, and men of violence take it by force. For all the prophets and the Law prophesied until John." The "kingdom of heaven," as he implies, is for the first time revealed as it is, *i.e.* as actually present, and men are pressing into it now that it has been revealed. The prophets spoke only of a future kingdom, living merely in the hope that somehow and at some time God would bring about the reign of righteousness upon the earth. Now men live in the glad consciousness that the reign of righteousness, which to the prophets seemed afar off, has actually begun. Hence Jesus speaks of the Baptist as having reached a higher stage of truth than the prophets. "Verily I say unto you, among them that are born of women, there hath not arisen a greater than John the Baptist." But he immediately adds: "Yet he that is but little in the kingdom of heaven is greater than he." So radical is the change introduced by the new revelation that it lifts those who accept it to a higher plane of truth than the Baptist, who still conceived of the kingdom of heaven as future, and who had not discovered the central truth that the kingdom of heaven was capable of being realised the moment it was discovered to consist in an unlimited love to God and man. Thus Jesus was perfectly aware that old things had passed away, and all things had become new. Nor had he any doubt of the absolute truth of his own doctrine. "All things have been delivered unto me of my Father; and no one knoweth the Son, save the Father, neither doth any know the Father save the Son, and he to whomsoever the Son willeth to reveal him." The revelation which he had to make to the world was an entirely new revelation. "Verily I say unto you that many prophets and righteous men have earnestly desired to see what ye see, and have not seen it, and to hear what ye hear and have not heard it." Yet, while he declares that his gospel is new, Jesus has too much insight into the presentiment of the truth, which half consciously worked in the highest minds of the past, not to be aware that the principle which he brought into the full light of day had been vaguely felt by religious men in all ages. The principle of evolution of which so much is now said has never been applied more precisely to the development of religious ideas than by Jesus.

The ideas of Jesus are all so closely connected, flowing as they do from a single principle, that it is impossible to treat of one aspect of his teaching without some reference to the other aspects. Hence it has not been possible to speak of his attitude towards the Law without to some extent anticipating what has now to be said in connexion with his attitude to the Messianic hopes of his countrymen. In what follows it will be advisable to consider this question in relation to (1) the general view of the scribes, (2) the higher view, rather felt than clearly formulated, by men of a more spiritual type. The points of agreement between these two classes of mind lay in the conviction that the world had been given over to wicked men and to the machinations of the devil and his angels; but that a time was coming when this state of things would be completely reversed, and a reign of righteousness set up upon the earth under the Messiah. But while there was a general agreement on these points, there was a radical difference in the conception of "righteousness," and as a consequence in the conception of the Messiah. Let us look first at the general view of the scribes and Pharisees.

(1) As we have already seen, their dissatisfaction with the evil of the present was closely connected with their legalistic ideas. To them it seemed that, by the terms of the covenant made between God and His own peculiar peo-

ple, Israel had a right to national independence, and even to sovereignty over all nations, as a reward for her devotion to Jehovah; or at least she was entitled to expect this reward when she fully implemented her part of the contract. Starting from this legal point of view, the evil of the present was explained as flowing from a failure to fulfil the terms of the covenant. God "does not exercise His kingship to its full extent, but on the contrary exposes His people to the heathen world-powers, to chastise them for their sins." By "sins" the Pharisees, of course, meant a want of conformity to the Law. Because of this disobedience, pain and sorrow prevailed, and especially those mental diseases which were directly referred to demoniac possession. For the same reason Israel groaned under the iron despotism of Rome. It is obvious that the future kingdom of God, which was to be ushered in by the Messiah, could only be conceived as consisting in the absence of pain and suffering, in dominion over the heathen, and in the rule of the saints, *i.e.* of those who were rigid in the practice of the Law.

Now the Pharisaic ideal of a kingdom of heaven, consisting in the absence of pain and suffering, in earthly sovereignty, and in the rule of Pharisaic saints, was one which Jesus could not possibly endorse. Denying *in limine* the whole conception upon which it rested, he could admit neither the Pharisaic conception of the present, nor their vulgar ideal of the future. The legalistic idea of a contract between God and Israel, the terms of which were that the pious Israelite who conformed to the letter of the Law had a right to freedom from suffering and to external sovereignty, was for him a profoundly immoral and irreligious conception; and the assumption that the government of God was not just and righteous was to him blasphemous. The world had never ceased to be the object of God's loving care, and therefore the coming of the kingdom of God could not mean a sudden and miraculous manifestation of His power. The spirit of God was present in the world of nature and in the consciousness of man. The obstacle to the reign of righteousness was in the blindness and sin of man, not in God. It was want of faith, and the sin which inevitably flowed from it, that explained the suffering and evil of the present.

We have seen how Jesus opposes to the legalism of the Pharisees his conception of a righteousness which consists in active efforts for the moral purification of the individual soul, a purification which could proceed only from love to God and man. Absolute faith in the goodness of God was the key-note of all his teaching. But if, as Jesus maintained, the essential nature of God is love for all creatures, and especially for man, how did he explain the existence of suffering and evil? How was the righteous government of God to be reconciled with the apparent triumph of evil? The optimism which shuts its eyes to the misery and wickedness of the world was to him a false and delusive creed. The wretchedness and evil of man were only too palpable. Jesus faced the facts with a perfectly clear consciousness of their force. No one was ever more sensitive to the sufferings of others than he; but he refused to see in suffering a proof of the indifference or injustice of God. His explanation of suffering was that it is a necessary step in the whole process by which man is lifted to a higher plane. To the Pharisees suffering was the result of the want of obedience to the Law, and therefore it seemed to them that, with the advent of the Messiah, and the destruction of all who transgressed the Law, suffering would disappear. Jesus also believes in the gradual disappearance of suffering, but he refuses to connect it with external conformity to the Law. The destruction of suffering must come from the efforts of loving hearts, not from any miraculous change in the conditions of human life. Suffering is not, or at least not merely, a punishment for sin, but a divinely ordained means for calling out the higher energies of the soul.

As in the view of the Pharisees suffering was the result of transgression of the Law, so also was the oppression of Israel by heathen powers. Hence they believed that, when the Messiah should come, the independence of Israel would be restored, and the whole world should come under the sway of "the saints."

Now, it has been maintained that Jesus, as an ardent patriot, shared in the hopes of his countrymen, and looked forward to the future sovereignty of Israel. This view cannot be accepted. For (*a*) even if Jesus cherished the hope of the external sovereignty of Israel, he could not possibly accept the ideal of the Pharisees. An Israel in which the whole government should be in the hands of "saints" of the Pharisaic type was something too dreadful to contemplate. No doubt Jesus was intensely patriotic in the sense of desiring that Israel should be the leader in the spiritual regeneration of the world, and it is probable that in the earlier days of his ministry he cherished the hope of persuading his countrymen to accept the new revelation. But, whether this was so or not, it is manifest that he came to see that the deep-rooted prejudices and externalism of the mass of the people, and the malignant opposition of the ruling classes, were too strong to be overcome. Recognising this clearly, it was impossible for him to believe that Israel should be raised to a supremacy over the heathen.

(*b*) Belief in the future rule of Israel was inseparably connected in the Jewish mind with the advent of a Messiah, who should ascend the throne of David and rule over a subject world. When, therefore, Jesus admitted to his disciples that the Messiah had already come in his own person, he plainly acknowledged that he had abandoned the whole set of ideas upon which the future political supremacy of Israel was based. The kingdom of heaven had already come, and it was not an earthly but a spiritual kingdom. In this kingdom he who was least was greatest, and indeed the spiritual power of the true Messiah — the power of loving service — was contrasted with the earthly power which consisted in ruling over a subject people. (*c*) While maintaining that the kingdom of heaven has already come, Jesus counsels submission to the established power of Rome, showing that in his mind the rule of righteousness was not dependent upon the political supremacy of Israel. His answer to the mother of Zebedee's children has been strangely cited as a proof that he looked forward to the earthly rule of the "saints." Nothing, in fact, could more clearly show that, in his mind, the kingdom of heaven was entirely independent of earthly power. To the naïve materialism of the good woman, who desired that her two sons should sit, one on his right hand and the other on his left, he answered: "Can ye be baptised with the baptism wherewith I have to be baptised?" In other words, he declares rank in the kingdom of heaven to consist in enlarged possibilities of loving service, not in outward pomp and sovereignty. And he significantly adds: "To sit on my right hand or on my left is not mine to give," *i.e.* the future is in the hands of God. The attitude of Jesus, as we may be sure, was one of such absolute trust in God, that he was quite prepared to accept the continued political dependence of Israel, if that were the will of God; and indeed towards the end of his life he seems to have seen perfectly clearly that the popular conception of the Messiah, which, in spite of all his efforts to turn it into a new channel, had taken firm hold upon the public mind, and was encouraged for their own ends by the Pharisees, could only result in the complete subjugation of Israel and the destruction of the temple service. In any case, the kingdom of heaven was so purely spiritual in its character that it could not possibly be connected in the mind of Jesus with the political supremacy of Israel. No doubt he wisely limited his efforts to "the lost sheep of the house of Israel," but this limitation was never in his mind connected with a belief in the future political sovereignty or even independence of Israel, but only with his ardent desire to secure the spiritual salvation of his countrymen, and through their instrumentality of the whole human race. The bitterness and hatred of the Pharisees, and of all who cherished ambitious hopes for the future of Israel, is largely explained by the way in which Jesus trampled upon all their cherished prejudices and political expectations. Not only did he tear off the garb of self-righteousness which they had wrapped around them; not only did he denounce them as enemies of true religion and morality; but he counselled what they regarded as a tame submission to the oppressive heathen power of Rome. Such a profound antagonism of ideals could only have one issue: the worldly material ideal must triumph for a time, only to be ultimately overcome by the intrinsically stronger ideal. Of this issue Jesus was clearly conscious, and therefore he warned his disciples that he would be the victim of the unholy rage of the rulers and their blind followers; while yet he announced with absolute confidence that the good cause would ultimately prevail. His optimism was therefore so profound and so robust, that even the worst expression of hatred and rancour did not destroy his faith. The passionate hatred with which he was pursued to the death was interpreted by him as a perversion of the inextinguishable desire for goodness which is inseparable from the consciousness of self. " Father, forgive them, for they know not what they do," is the expression of an optimism which rises triumphant over even the worst form of evil.

(2) The attitude of Jesus towards those pious souls who were disturbed by the apparent triumph of evil without and within,

was very different from the stern and uncompromising antagonism which he displayed toward the Pharisees. What disturbed the ordinary pious Jew was, not so much the prosperity of the *wicked*, as the prosperity of the *heathen*. Israel was the chosen people of God, and yet the "sinners of the Gentiles," *i.e.* the unholy nations, who had left Jehovah and given themselves up to idolatry and unclean rites, seemed to receive greater favour from God than the people whom He had chosen and who had remained faithful to Him. His special perplexity was the apparent injustice of God. A partial answer was no doubt found in the belief that God was chastising His people for their sins, and that He made use of the heathen, wicked as they were, as the instruments of His will. But the pious Jew never abandoned the belief that in some far-off time the favour of God would be restored to Israel, and that an awful day of reckoning would come for the heathen.

Now, Jesus does not absolutely deny that there is a certain justification in the contrast between the heathen and the Jew. To him also, the moral wickedness of the heathen and the grossness of their religious conceptions seem palpable; but he entirely denies the assumption that the Jew has any claim upon God to be freed from oppression, or that there is anything incompatible with the justice of God in the political oppression of Israel. The first assumption arises from conceiving of righteousness as obedience to an external law; the second, from a misapprehension of the true end of life. Hence he seeks to show that the course of the world is not to be explained on the legalistic supposition of an external system of rewards and punishments, or of a special claim on the part of the Jew to the favour of God. The righteous man has no *right* to an external reward for his righteousness; the Jew has no claim *as* a Jew to the favour of God. For the end of human life is not external prosperity, but the development of the spirit. When this is once admitted, the difficulty arising from the apparent triumph of the wicked assumes an entirely new aspect. External prosperity is no test of spiritual elevation. "What shall it profit a man if he gains the whole world and loses his life?" The true nature of man is seen, not in his desire for the perishable things of this world, but in "hunger and thirst after righteousness." Nothing can satisfy man but the growth in him of the divine spirit, and he in whom that spirit dwells is not disturbed by the want of those things which are the mere accidents of existence, not its essence. What is called the prosperity of the wicked is not true prosperity. This is the idea which Jesus enforces in that part of the Sermon on the Mount which he seems to have addressed to those who came to hear him, attracted by something kindred in themselves. "Lay not up for yourselves treasures upon earth; but lay up for yourselves treasures in heaven." The true life does not consist in the attainment of finite and limited ends, but in the possession of that which is eternal and imperishable. The beginning of spiritual life, therefore, consists in an entire surrender of the finite. But this is only the negative side of his teaching: the positive side is the direction of the whole being to the infinite and eternal, or the laying up of "treasures in heaven." This, of course, does not mean that man is to separate himself from all earthly concerns, and set his affections upon the future life, in the sense of looking forward to a reward which it is hopeless to expect in the present life. The "heavenly treasures" do not consist in outward qualifications, either there or here, but in a "change of mind," which transforms the whole spirit, and throws a new light upon all things. "If thine eye be single, thy whole body shall be full of light." So when the "mind's eye" is single, the whole world assumes a new aspect. This transformation of the soul is the new creation of the world: the mind to which everything seemed an insoluble riddle now sees the confused and indistinct mass of objects fall into their proper place in the organic unity of the whole. All finite ends are universalised when they are viewed by reference to God, and all worthy action is then seen to consist in the service of God. "Ye cannot serve God and mammon."

Now, if the true life of man consists in the service of God, the wicked must not be regarded as prosperous, but as miserable in the extreme. They have lost what Dante calls the "good of the intellect,"— that rational good which is the source of all joy and peace. There can be no need to "justify the ways of God" by any far-fetched attempt to explain why wickedness is rewarded and righteousness punished. Wickedness is *never* rewarded, and righteousness is *never* punished. It is no reward to "lose one's life": it is no punishment to "save one's life." For he who seeks the lower misses the higher, while he who seeks the higher has the lower "added to him." In other words, devotion to universal or impersonal ends — to all that makes for the good of the whole — is the secret of blessedness. By giving up his exclusive self man gains a wider self, which is the true self. And this true self is but another name for life in God. For the only reason why in this higher life man is in unity with himself is because he is in unity with the whole tendency of the world, *i.e.* with the will of God.

In his earlier teaching Jesus seeks to commend the new way of truth by showing that the love of God is revealed in nature as well as in human life. We have seen how, in later Judaism, the decay of prophetic inspiration and devotion to the letter of the Law resulted in ultimately making God a name for an indefinable Power, not revealed in the world, but concealed behind an impenetrable veil. Thus the tendency, which was always present in the Jewish religion, reached its climax. Now Jesus entirely reverses this conception of a purely transcendent God. God is indeed the Creator of the world, but He is best seen, not in the great and terrible forces of nature, but in its silent and orderly processes, and in the purposive energy which works in the life of flower and bird and beast. He does not stand apart from nature in lonely isolation, but His spirit pervades all things and quickens them by its presence. Hence in his parables Jesus finds the evidence of

God's goodness in the ordinary occurrences of the homely earth. There is a tender and solemn light on the most familiar things because God is felt to be present in them, not hidden behind them. Especially in the life and growth of nature Jesus finds evidence of the continuous and loving care of God. With penetrative imagination he sees the formative activity of God working in the beauty with which He clothes the grass of the field, which to-day is and to-morrow is cast into the oven; in the lilies, clothed in a glory exceeding all the splendour of human art; in the insignificant mustard-seed, which expands in harmony with all the skyey influences into the organic unity of root, stem, leaves, and blossoms, with the birds swaying in its branches. Thus God works not *upon* but *through* the things which have come from His hands. Nature is not a dead machine, wielded by the hands of omnipotence, but it is instinct with that eternal principle of life which exhibits itself in the ever-recurring cycle of changes, inorganic and organic. To the eye of Jesus, nature is thus a manifestation of the wisdom and loving care of God; and he asks if it is credible that He who takes such pains to fashion and provide for the life of plant and animal is less interested in man. "Behold, the birds of the heaven, that they sow not, neither do they reap, nor gather into barns, and your heavenly Father feedeth them. Are not ye of much more value than they?"

The "free and friendly eyes" with which Jesus in the earlier years of his ministry contemplated nature never deserted him; but, as the malevolence and opposition of the scribes and Pharisees with their blinded followers increased, the problem of evil demanded even a deeper faith. There was to him no real trial of faith in the external prosperity of the wicked, for he saw that the wicked received precisely the reward which their acts demanded; but the apparent success of the opposition to the work of God seemed to demand another explanation. Having absolute faith in the saving power of love, he yet found that in the majority of his countrymen his revelation only provoked a more bigoted belief in their own unspiritual ideas and a hatred of the truth that was growing in intensity until, as he foresaw, the sacrifice of his own life would be the inevitable result. A similar result, it was evident to him, must follow the diffusion of the truth in all ages. The conflict of principles must ever call into play all that is best and all that is worst in man. "Think not that I came to send peace on the earth: I came not to send peace, but a sword." How is this weakness of the good cause to be explained? Has God in truth, as the majority believed, given over the world to the rule of Satan?

The answer of Jesus reveals the infinite depth of his optimism. The triumph of the evil cause is no triumph, but a defeat. For in what does it consist? It cannot kill the truth itself, which is eternal, but only the body of those whose lives are a witness of its power. There is nothing in life so pathetic as the temporary triumph of a bad cause; for that triumph means that for a time men in their delusion are shut out from the blessedness of unity with God, and therefore with themselves. On the other hand, those who live in the truth have the whole tendency of things on their side, and conscious of this they cannot be touched in the centre of their being. Still the problem remains: why does evil apparently triumph? A partial answer is, that its triumph is only apparent—it is never complete, and it has no permanency. But more than this: its temporary triumph is essential to the full disclosure of all that the truth contains. The false principle must show its bitter fruits, and must accomplish its perfect work before it completely reveals its true nature. Hence, the more it outwardly triumphs and shows its evil nature, the more surely is the way prepared for its final overthrow. "Where the carcase is, there are the vultures gathered together." Man *can* only seek for truth and goodness, and if for a time he turns his energies against the good cause, it is not in the spirit of a being who desires evil—for man is not a devil, but in his real being a "son of God"—but in his confusion of the true with the false. Hence the outward success of the bad cause is a real failure. Just as man cannot find rest in any finite end, so he can never be satisfied permanently with anything short of the truth. It is the truth he is really seeking, and at last the truth must prevail. Thus Jesus finds in the worst form of evil a "soul of goodness." The world is through and through the product of divine love.

Now, with this grasp of the principle that the good cause must ultimately prevail, while yet it implies a conflict with the opposite principle of evil, Jesus saw that the kingdom of heaven was a process, a development of the higher in its struggle with the lower. Nothing can ultimately withstand the principle of goodness; but in his blindness and evil will man may for a time turn his energies against it. Hence the slow growth of the "kingdom of heaven,"—a growth so slow that it often seems to be arrest or even retrogression. This idea is expressed by Jesus in a variety of figures. The kingdom of heaven is compared to the leaven, which was "hid in three measures of meal till the whole was leavened." The most striking expression of the idea, however, is given in that wonderful parable preserved in the oldest of the gospels, the gospel of Mark: "So is the kingdom of heaven as if a man should cast seed into the ground, and should sleep and rise day and night, and the seed should spring and grow up, he knoweth not how. For the earth bringeth forth fruit of herself; first the blade, then the ear, then the full corn in the ear. But when the fruit is ripe, immediately he putteth in the sickle, for the harvest is come."

The attitude of Jesus towards the Messianic hope of his countrymen at once follows from his conception of the kingdom of heaven as already present, and yet as a process of conflict with evil. Holding these views he could not possibly believe in any sudden or miraculous change which should break the continuity between the present and the future. Hence he refused to attest his divine mission by signs and wonders. When the Pharisees, in their usual crass materialism, demanded a "sign,"— *i.e.* demanded that Jesus should virtually deny the presence of God in the ordinary processes of nature and in the normal experiences of human life — his answer was: "An evil and adulterous generation seeketh after a sign, and there shall no sign be given to it but the sign of the prophet Jonah." What he meant was, as Luke saw, that no "sign" could authenticate his mission but the truth which he proclaimed. Truth "shines by its own light," and if men "will not hear Moses and the prophets, neither would they believe if one were to rise from the dead." Hence Jesus, though he employs the apocalyptic imagery current in his day, entirely transforms the current conception of the future success of the kingdom of heaven. The triumph of good over evil, as he affirms, is not to be effected by catastrophe and revolution, but only by the persistent labours of those who live in the truth. His faith does not rest upon a superstitious belief in a sudden interposition from heaven. In his eyes good can be developed only through the loving efforts of those in whom the divine Spirit operates, and who "let their light so shine among men that others, seeing their good works, glorify their Father which is in heaven." Thus his optimism flows from absolute trust in the goodness of God, and in a recognition that man in his ideal nature is a "son of God." For this reason he believes that to the success of the kingdom it is essential that each individual should have a personal experience of the truth. This is indicated by the images of the leaven and the mustard-seed. He does not expect the triumph of goodness from any external arrangements of society, or rather he conceives of these as but the partial expression of a truth which must first exist in those whose hearts are open to the truth. At the same time, since the very essence of Jesus' teaching is the essentially social nature of man, the principle which he announced could not but manifest itself in a transformation of social and political institutions, though these can never be more than a partial expression of the idea of a kingdom in which the spirit of God is present in each member of the whole, at once distinguishing and uniting them in an organic unity.

In this conception of a spiritual community, in which each has found himself by losing himself, Jesus finds the answer to that longing for deliverance from the evil of their own hearts which was the saving salt in the aspirations of the pious souls of his own day. Just as he refuses to postpone the kingdom of heaven to some far-off day, when good shall conquer evil, maintaining that evil is already overcome in principle; so he tells those who "labour and are heavy-laden," longing for a deliverance in which they have but faint belief, that the way to the conquest of evil in themselves is now open. And the secret is in identification with their brethren, the sons of the one Father. This was the secret of that triumphant optimism which nothing could destroy in him. This idea is expressed in the title which he most frequently applied to himself, the "Son of Man." This term is often used in the Old Testament,—for instance, in Ezekiel,—to express the weakness and dependence of man, as contrasted with the power and majesty of God. In Daniel, again, it refers not to a personal Messiah, but to the collective body of the saints, as contrasted with the great, victorious beasts, the symbols of the powerful world-empires. "The core of Daniel's Messianic hope is the universal dominion of the saints."* Now if, as seems probable, Jesus adopted the term from Daniel, he meant by it to indicate, not merely the spirituality of his kingdom, but his own identity with the whole race. In any case, the essential meaning of the title is that Jesus conceived himself as part and parcel of humanity: in other words, he found the secret of life in complete identification with its joys and sorrows, its successes and sins. And because he was thus identified with man, he is also called the "Son of God." He was one with the Father in nature, though not in person, since he was conscious of himself as the medium through which the eternal love of God was revealed and communicated to men. Nothing can, in his view, withstand the power of love. Man, weak and sinful as he is, must succumb to the omnipotence of goodness, for goodness is the spirit of the living God. It was with a full sense of the importance of

---

* Schürer's *History of the Jewish People*, 2. 2. 138.

the question that, towards the close of his life, he asked the disciples: "Who do ye say that the Son of Man is?" And when Peter, in a flash of insight, answered: "Thou art the Christ, the Son of the living God," he immediately goes on to warn the disciples that he must "suffer many things of the elders and chief priests and the scribes, and be killed." He was the Messiah, just because it was his mission to effect the deliverance of mankind, not through outward triumph, but through suffering and death. To the disciples, with their preconception of a Messiah who should come invested with miraculous power and dignity, this was a "hard saying"; and the same apostle, who had for a moment got a glimpse of the divine humanity of Jesus, now exclaims in horror: "Be it far from thee, Lord: this shall never be unto thee." Thus even Peter puts himself on the side of those who imagined that a suffering Messiah was a contradiction in terms. He had not learned the lesson of the divine life and teaching of the Master, and therefore Jesus rebukes him for the materialism of his conception: "Thou art a stumbling-block unto me: for thou mindest not the things of God, but the things of men." It is not by self-assertion and outward triumph, but by suffering and death, that the true Christ and his followers can save the world: "Whosoever would save his life shall lose it: and whosoever shall lose his life for my sake shall gain it."

As he transforms the ordinary idea of the Messiah, so Jesus gives to the belief in a final judgment of the world a new and deeper meaning. The wicked and the righteous are no longer distinguished as those who obey the law from those who violate it, but as those who love from those who are indifferent to their fellow-men. The whole system of external rewards and punishments is swept away, and in its place we have the one fundamental distinction of those whose lives are ruled by the spirit of brotherhood, and those who live for themselves. Under the guise of the current imagery of a Last Judgment, when all men shall be gathered together to receive their final sentence, Jesus inculcates the truth that the spiritual status of men is already determined by the principle which is outwardly expressed in their actions. "Inasmuch as ye did it unto one of these my brethren, even these least, ye did it unto me." Thus while he leaves untouched the current belief in a future judgment, he brings to the test of human action an entirely new standard. Not the pious works upon which men pride themselves, but the unselfish life, determines the eternal destiny of man. He who lives the divine life is he who, like the Master, has merged his own good in the good of the whole, and who has proved his love of man by the ordinary tender charities which seem so little, but mean so much.

From what has been said we can understand the sense in which Jesus speaks of "Faith." To the scribes and Pharisees religion meant acceptance of the teaching of the doctors of the Law, as based upon their interpretations of scripture. Thus for the ordinary Jew there was a double wall of partition raised between him and God. Not only had he no direct consciousness of the divine nature, and therefore of his own nature, but even the revelations of truth which were contained in scripture came to him through the distorted medium of tradition. No doubt it was impossible to read the inspired words of legislator and prophet without catching something of their spirit; but so overlaid was the sacred text with the prosaic and deadening interpretations of the scribes, which were dinned into his ears at home, at school, and in the synagogue, that it was hard for him to pierce through the mass of traditional ideas to the truth which they overlaid and obscured. One consequence of this traditionalism was an incapacity to judge for himself when a new revelation of truth was presented to him. This was one of the great obstacles which Jesus met in his effort to bring his countrymen into living contact with the truth. The leaden weight of custom lay heavy upon the minds of "the people of the Law," and only by a powerful effort could they shake off the mass of prejudice and superstition which they had been taught to regard as the revelation of God. And this intellectual difficulty was intensified by the spiritual arrogance which had been engendered in their minds by the traditional belief in their unique position as the people of Jehovah. Thus the Jew had to free both his intellect and his conscience from the fetters of traditionalism before he was in a position to look straight at the truth. This explains why Jesus insists upon "faith" as a child-like attitude. Only those from whose minds and hearts the artificial veil of custom and pride of race had been removed were in a position to accept the new revelation of truth. It is in this sense, and not in the sense of unreasoning credulity, that he commends the "faith" of those who welcomed the truth. Thus for him "faith" is that openness to light which is a form of reason; it is, in fact, reason in its purest form. What Jesus called upon men to believe he supported, not by an appeal to authority, but by an appeal to truth itself. He asked them to look with open eyes at the evidences of God's goodness as exhibited in the world of nature; to examine their own hearts, and to read the sayings of the holy men of old with intelligence and insight. To the persistent demand for supernatural "signs" of his divine mission, he refused to listen, seeing in them but another form of that crude materialism which infected all their ideas. A saving "faith" he found in those few whose consciousness of their own weakness and sinfulness was so strong that, under the influence of his life and words, it removed the mist of tradition from their minds, and overcame the racial pride so natural in a Jew. "Faith" is thus that union of intellectual candour and moral simplicity which flows from the vision of God. It cannot be transferred externally from one person to another, but is possible only in him who has surrendered all that ministers to self-righteousness and selfishness. It is thus another name for the consciousness of unity and reconciliation with God, and for that "enthusiasm of humanity" which flows from it. "Faith," in other words, is the personal side of the whole consciousness of the "kingdom of heaven," as Jesus understood it: it is the spirit which operates in every member of those who are reconciled with God, and are therefore at unity with themselves and with one another.

No doubt this faith has various degrees, but in essence it is always the same. It is also recognised by Jesus that it grows from age to age; for, while he speaks of the Law and the prophets as giving a revelation of the divine nature, he also maintains that he has himself given a higher revelation of God than was possible to them. " Many prophets and righteous men have earnestly desired to see what ye see and have not seen it, and to hear what ye hear and have not heard it." Here, as always, Jesus holds by both sides of the truth: the essential identity of the religious consciousness in all ages, and the process of expansion which it undergoes as it comes to a fuller consciousness of what it contained implicitly from the first.

There is one other aspect of Christ's teaching which must not be passed over. Although the Messianic hope was usually connected in the Jewish mind with the appearance of an earthly Messiah, and the resurrection of the dead for judgment, it was also held by many that after the long reign of the saints there should follow an eternity of bliss or woe in another world. Now, although Jesus gave a new meaning to the kingdom of heaven, and insisted that it already existed in the consciousness of those who were reconciled to God and devoted to the good of humanity, he also held the doctrine of personal immortality. When the Sadducees came, demanding a proof of immortality, he appealed to the words of scripture: "I am the God of Abraham and the God of Isaac and the God of Jacob," adding that "God is not the God of the dead but of the living." There was an especial appropriateness in this reply as directed against the Sadducees, who prided themselves upon being faithful to the teaching of scripture, as distinguished from the traditional interpretation accepted by the Pharisees. But, as we have seen, Jesus does not accept even the teaching of the "Law and the prophets" without first bringing to bear upon it the light of his own higher consciousness, and hence we may be certain that these words were more than an *argumentum ad hominem*, intended to silence the

Sadducees. The meaning of Jesus seems to be that, as the consciousness of the living God involves the consciousness of man as identical in his essential nature with God, we must believe in the eternal continuance of this fundamental relation. To see what man is in his true nature is to know that his life comes from God, and that only in the consciousness of his union with God does he learn what in essence he is. The essence of man is his life, *i.e.* his conscious existence, and this must be as eternal as God. The true destiny of man is to live in union with God, and this destiny cannot be taken from him by God whose son he is. Thus Jesus, as he conceives of God as the ever-living Father, also conceives of men as beings with an immortal destiny. The future existence of man he also conceives as a higher stage of being, when they shall be "as the angels," *i.e.* shall enjoy a clearer vision of God, and when goodness shall at last have overcome evil, and no longer be forced to engage in perpetual conflict with it. While Jesus thus maintains the personal immortality of man, he does not base upon it a proof of the reality of his view of life; on the contrary, he bases immortality upon the belief in God and the essential identity in nature of God and man. For he asserts that those who will not be convinced of the truth by "Moses and the prophets" would not believe "even if one were to rise from the dead." The order of ideas in his mind therefore is God, sonship, immortality. It is our knowledge of the nature of God which reveals to us his Fatherhood, and his Fatherhood is the proof of the immortality of his children.

CHAPTER V

MEDIÆVAL CHRISTIANITY

In the last chapter an attempt has been made to present the Christian ideal of life, as set forth by its Founder. No attempt will here be made to deal with that imposing edifice of doctrine which was built up by St. Paul and the other apostles and by the subsequent reflection of Christian theologians; but it will help to throw the teaching of Jesus into bolder relief, if we contrast with it the Christianity of the Middle Ages.

When we pass from the religion of Jesus to mediæval Christianity, we seem to have entered into another world. The free and genial glance with which our Lord contemplated nature, the triumphant optimism of his conception of human life, and his absolute faith in the realisation of the kingdom of heaven here and now, have been replaced by a hard and almost mechanical idea of the external world, by a stern denunciation of the utter perversity and evil of society, and by the postponement of the kingdom of heaven to the future life. How has this remarkable change come over the Christian consciousness? To answer this question would be a long task, and I shall only state three main characteristics in the mediæval conception of life, trying to indicate how they originated.

(1) The first characteristic to which I shall refer is the universal belief that the "kingdom of heaven," to use the term which Jesus so often employs, could not be realised in this life, but was entirely a thing of the future life. We can trace the gradual growth of this conviction. The crucifixion of their Lord was a terrible shock to his disciples, and there is good reason to believe that for a moment it caused their belief in his Messiahship to waver. But, as the divine life and sayings of the Master came back to their remembrance, they began to understand what he had him-

self always affirmed—that his kingdom was a spiritual one, which could be realised only by the destruction of evil and the triumph of righteousness. Yet they still clung to the idea that so great a revolution could be accomplished only by a sudden and miraculous change; and hence in the Apostolic Age the Christian, imperfectly liberated from the materialism of the ordinary Messianic conception, imagined that the complete triumph of righteousness would take place in a few years by the second coming of the Lord to establish upon earth the reign of peace and good will. Living in this faith, the primitive community of Christians made no attempt to interfere with existing institutions, civil or ecclesiastical, but were content to prepare for the imminent advent of the Lord. But as time went on, and still the Lord did not appear, his advent came to seem more and more remote. Meantime the Christian found himself living in the midst of the decaying civilisation of Rome, and there was little wonder that the conversion of the world should seem an almost impossible task:—

> Stout was its arm, each thew and bone
> Seemed puissant and alive,—
> But ah! its heart, its heart was stone,
> And so it could not thrive.

"How can these bones live?" he naturally exclaimed. How can this mass of corruption be transformed into the divine image? Moreover, try as they might to avoid collision with the secular power of the Roman empire, the Christians found that they could not meet together for mutual encouragement and stimulation, without drawing suspicion upon themselves as a secret society plotting the overthrow of the empire; and, indeed, though they had no such purpose, the Christian ideal was antagonistic to the pagan, and must at last meet with and overcome it, or be itself subdued. The outward symbol of this war of ideals was the persecutions to which the Christians were subjected in the second and third centuries. Thus the present world came to appear more and more a wilderness through which the little band of Christians was compelled to march, sad and solitary, on their way to the heavenly land. This sombre cast of thought never vanished from the Christian consciousness till the modern age, and perhaps it cannot be said to have quite vanished even now. One might have supposed that the more hopeful spirit of an earlier age would have come back when Christianity had, by its resistless energy, compelled the Roman empire, in the person of Constantine, to make terms with it. But the inrush of the fierce northern hordes into the Roman empire, and their facile conversion to Christianity, confirmed in a new way the "otherworldliness" of the Church. For Christianity, to their rude and undisciplined minds, was in all its deeper aspects unintelligible, and its doctrines could only be accepted in blind and unquestioning faith. A superstitious reverence for the Church did not restrain them from the wildest excesses of passion, and the only curb to their brutal violence and self-will was the hope of future reward or the dread of future retribution. Thus mediæval Christianity, unable to overcome the barbarism and lawlessness of the world, in a sort of despair sought comfort in the future life.

This is the spirit which rules the whole of the Middle Ages, and it was one of the tasks of the Reformation to awaken anew the consciousness of the infinite significance of the present life as a preparation for the future life, and to quicken all the institutions of society and all the powers of the individual soul with the divine spirit of pristine Christianity.

(2) A second characteristic of the mediæval period is a belief in the absolute authority of the Church in all matters of faith and worship, and the consequent distinction between the clergy and the laity. This idea had its roots in the same principle as that which led to the conception of religion as essentially the hope of a future world. The rude barbarian could not comprehend the doctrines of the Church, nor could his self-will be broken except by a power to which he was forced to bend his stubborn will. Hence the Church demanded implicit faith in its teaching, and absolute submission to its authority. Nor is it easy to see how otherwise the soil could have been prepared in which the new seed of the Reformation was to grow. The

discipline of the mediæval Church was, on the whole, as salutary as it was inevitable; but discipline is justifiable only as a preparation for the exercise of independence and reason; and hence the time inevitably came when men, having outgrown the stage of pupilage, asserted their indefeasible right to a rational liberty. This was the claim made by Luther when he unfurled "the banner of the free spirit."

(3) The last characteristic of the Middle Ages to which I shall refer is the opposition of faith and reason. To come to its full rights as the universal religion Christianity had to free itself from all that was accidental and temporary in the conceptions of its first adherents. The first step in this process was taken when St. Paul disengaged it from the accidents of its Jewish origin and presented its essence in a clear and definite form. But the process could not end here, for every age has its own preconceptions and its own difficulties. When Christianity went beyond the boundaries of Judea, it had to meet and overcome the dualism of Greek thought, as it had met and overcome Jewish narrowness and ex-

clusiveness. The victory was only imperfectly accomplished. The reconciling principle of the essential identity of the human and divine could not be abandoned without the destruction of the central idea of Christianity, but the Church did not entirely escape the danger of making theology a transcendent theory of the absolutely inscrutable nature of God. At this imperfect stage of development Christian dogma was for a time arrested, so that when reflection arose with Scholasticism the doctrines of the Church were assumed to be expressions of absolute truth, although they contained certain mysterious and incomprehensible elements. There is indeed in the development of Scholasticism itself a growing consciousness of the antagonism of reason to the dogmas of the Church as commonly understood, a consciousness which in Occam even reaches the form of a belief that there are doctrines which are not only "beyond" but "contrary to" reason; but the schoolmen never lost their faith in the truth of the dogmas, though they passed from *credo ut intelligam* to *intelligo ut credam*, and ended with *credo quia impossible*. When it thus came to be explicitly affirmed that the doctrines of the Church contained not merely *super*rational but *ir*rational elements, the beginning of the end was near; for reason, frustrated in its attempt to find unity with itself in an authoritative creed, could only fall back in despair upon a universal scepticism or set about a reconstruction of the creed itself. Thus Scholasticism dug its own grave as well as the grave of mediæval theology, and prepared the way for that great modern movement which began with the Renaissance and the Reformation and is still going on. Of one thing we may be sure, that nothing short of a perfect harmony of science, art, and religion can permanently satisfy the liberated human spirit. At such a harmony it is the hard task of philosophy to aim, and only in so far as it is secured can we hope for the return of that half-vanished faith in the omnipotence of goodness with which Jesus was so abundantly filled. It is therefore proposed, in the second part of this work, to ask how far an idealistic philosophy enables us to retain the fundamental conception of life which was enunciated by the Founder of Christianity.

PART II

MODERN IDEALISM IN ITS RELATION TO THE CHRISTIAN IDEAL OF LIFE

CHAPTER VI

GENERAL STATEMENT AND DEFENCE OF IDEALISM

IN his *Foundations of Belief*, Mr. Balfour raises an objection to the idealistic theory of knowledge, a consideration of which may help to bring out more clearly what is here meant by Idealism. This objection is directed primarily against what is claimed to be the doctrine of the late T. H. Green, but it is thought to apply with equal force against all who hold the idealistic view of the world. In what follows no attempt will be made to defend Green from Mr. Balfour's attack. It does not appear to me true that Green reduced the world to a "network of relations"; but it seems better to avoid all disputes which turn upon the interpretation of an author who is not here to defend himself, and therefore I shall deal from an independent point of view with the difficulty which Mr. Balfour has stated with his usual force and clearness.

The main charge made by Mr. Balfour against Idealism is that it "reduces all experience to an experience of relations," or "constitutes the universe out of categories." Now, it is no doubt true, says our author, that we cannot reduce the universe to "an unrelated chaos of impressions or sensations"; but "must we not also grant that in all experience there is a refractory element which, though it cannot be presented in isolation, nevertheless refuses wholly to merge its being in a network of relations?" If so, whence does this irreducible element arise? The mind, we are told, is the source of relations. What is the source of that which is related? The "thing in itself" of Kant "raises more difficulties than it solves," and indeed, the followers of Kant themselves point out that this hypothetical cause of that which is "given" in experience cannot be known as a cause, or even as existing. But "we do not get rid of the difficulty by getting rid of Kant's solution of it. His dictum still seems to remain true, that 'without matter categories are empty.' And, indeed, it is hard to see how it is possible to conceive a universe in which nothing is to be permitted for the relations to subsist between. Relations surely imply a something which is related, and if that something is, in the absence of relations, 'nothing for us as thinking beings,' so relations in the absence of that something are mere symbols emptied of their signification."*

Mr. Balfour, it would seem, rejects the sensationalist theory that knowledge is reducible to an association of individual feelings, and he also rejects the Kantian reference of impressions of sense to a "thing in itself"; but he is unable to see how the world can be explained without the retention of a "matter" to supply the concrete filling for the otherwise empty categories. His own view would therefore seem to be that the knowable world involves two distinct elements, a "matter of sense" and the conceptions or relations by which that "matter" is

* Balfour's *Foundations of Belief.* Am. ed., pp. 144–5.

formed. Where he differs from Idealism, as he understands it, is in denying that all reality can be reduced to relations of thought or pure conceptions. The force of Mr. Balfour's criticism, therefore, depends upon two assumptions: firstly, that it is possible to retain the Kantian doctrine of a "matter of sense" after the rejection of Kant's assumption of a "thing in itself"; and, secondly, that Idealism seeks to construct the world out of empty conceptions or relations of thought. Both of these assumptions I venture to challenge.

(1) The Kantian doctrine of a "matter of sense" stands or falls with the assumption of a "thing in itself." In the *Æsthetic* the problem of knowledge is put by Kant in this way: What is the element in the perception of objects as in space and time which belongs to the subject, and what is the element which belongs to the object? Kant's answer is, that the "form" under which objects are related spatially and temporally is due to the subject, the "matter" so related to the object. Now, in this contrast of "form" and

"matter," it is obviously assumed that the subject has a nature of its own independently of the object, and the object a nature of its own independently of the subject; in other words, that, *as existences*, subject and object are unrelated to each other. On the other hand it is admitted by Kant that there can be no *knowledge* until the subject comes into relation to the object.

Now, the assumption of the independent existence of subject and object is no doubt a very natural assumption, because, when we begin to explain knowledge, we already have knowledge. But we must not forget that, in accounting for the origin of knowledge, we have no right to assume the very knowledge we are seeking to explain. We cannot start from the independent existence of subject and object unless we can show that an independent subject and object can be known. Before we ask what is contributed by the subject, and what comes from the object, we must be sure that the separation of subject and object is admissible. If there is no known subject which does not imply a known object, the element belonging to the one cannot be separated from the element belonging to the other. When Kant asks "by what means our faculty of knowledge should be aroused to activity but by objects," he forgets that neither object nor subject exists for knowledge prior to knowledge, and that to ask how the subject should be "aroused to activity" by the object is to ask how a non-existent object should act upon a non-existent subject. This question cannot be answered, because it is self-contradictory, for to a self-contradictory question no answer can possibly be given.

But though Kant starts from the opposition of subject and object, he takes, in the *Æsthetic*, the first step to effect its overthrow. The *real* object, he says, no doubt exists apart from the subject, but the *known* object does not. For, in the perception of objects, the relations of space and time are the manner in which the subject, when "aroused to activity," comes to have a consciousness of objects. So far, therefore, as knowledge goes, the object is not an independent existence, but an existence in and for a conscious subject. Now this view leads to an important change in our ordinary conception of the world. When we assume an objective world, fully formed and complete in itself, apart from the subject, we manifestly make the subject a mere passive spectator of a world from which it stands apart; and when we assume a subject with a complex nature of its own, we make the world entirely foreign to the subject. But the moment we ask how this objective world becomes known to the subject, we find that the independence of each alternately disappears in the other. Thus, if the object is apprehended by the subject, and only in this apprehension exists for it, the whole objective world is absorbed into the subject. On the other hand, if we ask what is the content of the subject, we find that it is the object, and thus the subject is absorbed in the object. Kant, however, does not carry over the object as a whole into the subject, but draws a distinction between the element which comes from the object and the element which is added by the subject. In this way the identification of subject and object is partially arrested, and an intermediate region is assumed in which subject and object enter into relation with each other. This is the region of knowledge. But, while this union of subject and object is the condition of knowable reality, subject and object still remain apart as existences. Here, then, we have the "thing in itself," as it appears in the *Æsthetic*.

The compromise which Kant here adopts is obviously untenable. If we are to assume the independent existence of subject and object, we must not at the same time assume that the one is dependent for its reality upon the other. Since the spatial and temporal relations have a meaning only within knowledge, they can no more belong to the subject than to the object, but only to the subject in so far as there has arisen for it the consciousness of an object determinable under those relations. Why, then, does Kant maintain that space and time are forms of perception, not determinations of the real? He does so because he has not completely freed himself from the dualism of subject and object with which he starts. A subject assumed to exist apart from the object must be regarded as a pure blank so far as knowledge is concerned; and when it begins to know we must suppose it to be affected by the object. Thus it is regarded as purely receptive in its relation to the object, and therefore it has to wait for the action of the object upon it. Now when we ask whether the subject can be purely receptive, or whether it must not be affirmed to be at once receptive and conscious of being receptive, it becomes manifest that the whole conception of a purely receptive subject is unmeaning. If the subject is receptive without being aware of it, it will simply exist in a series of individual states, without referring those states either to an object or to itself. For such a subject there can be no objective world; for, as Kant himself tells us, the consciousness of objects implies "the reference of sensation to objects in perception." On the other hand, if the subject not only exists in a series of affections, but is conscious of affections as coming from the object, it must distinguish them as its own and yet relate them to the object. But so far as it does so, the object is within knowledge, not a thing existing by itself. Thus the object has no existence for the subject except as the subject distinguishes it from and yet relates it to itself. The object is the product of its own activity, and hence the subject cannot be receptive in regard to it. A subject which is not self-active is for itself nothing. In truth, a purely receptive subject is a contradiction in terms. It is only because Kant does not distinguish between a subject which is purely sensitive — and only by an abuse of language can this be called a "subject" at all — and a subject which is conscious of its states as involving permanent relations, that he allows himself to speak of the subject as receptive in relation to the object. Whatever the object is, it is for a subject, and any other object is a fiction of abstraction. We may legitimately contrast the object as known in fuller determinateness with the object as less determinate, but the object is in either case a known object, not a "thing in itself." To contrast a known with an unknown object is the greatest of all absurdities, because an unknown object is simply nothing for the subject, and therefore cannot be contrasted with anything.

It follows from what has been said that there can be no opposition between the "matter" and the "form" of knowledge: no opposition, that is, between a "matter" which comes from the object and a "form" contributed by the subject. We must therefore deny that affections of sense as such enter into or form any element in knowable objects. Kant himself admits that such affections do not exist as an object for consciousness, but are merely the "manifold" out of which objects are formed: they are the "matter" which becomes an object, when the subject combines its determinations under the form of time into an image or perception. But when the "manifold of sense" becomes an object, it is no longer a "matter" to which the subject has to give "form," but is already a formed matter. The subject does not first receive the "matter of sense," and then impose upon it its own forms; only in so far as the "matter" is already formed does it exist for the subject at all. The so-called "manifold of sense" is therefore just the distinguishable aspects of the world as these exist for the conscious subject. This world is indeed "manifold" in the sense of being infinitely concrete; but its concreteness is not that of an aggregate of particulars, but of a "cosmos of experience," in which all the particulars distinguished are held together in the unity of a single world, which exists only for a combining self-active subject.

(2) The denial of the fiction of a "matter of sense," entirely destitute of the unifying activity of intelligence, is therefore a very different thing from the denial of all differences and the reduction of reality to a "network of relations." Mr. Balfour's charge that Idealism reduces the world to relations, and therefore involves the absurdity of relations with nothing to relate, rests upon a misunderstanding of the idealistic theory of thought or intelligence as the constitutive principle of all knowledge and all reality. What Ideal-

ism maintains is that the knowable world exists only for a thinking or self-conscious subject, and that even the simplest phase of knowledge involves the activity of that subject. It is very inadequate and misleading to speak of thought as if it consisted solely in the relation of separate elements to one another. When thought is thus conceived, it is easy to understand why those who affirm that the world exists only for thought are supposed to be constructing reality out of pure abstractions. It is not difficult to show that this conception is a survival of the old untenable opposition of perception and thought, as dealing respectively with the particular and the universal. Let us take a simple case by way of illustration. I perceive a speck of light in the surrounding darkness. Taking the old abstract view, we have here the simple apprehension of a particular sensible object, without any exercise of the activity of thought. The latter comes into play only when I compare various perceptions with each other. Such a doctrine was virtually disposed of when Kant showed that the simplest perception already involves the synthetic activity of thought. My apprehension of the speck of light is by no means simple. The moment I have the sensation, my mind goes to work, seeking to put it in its proper place in relation to the rest of my experience. There are no doubt occasions in my individual life in which this interpretative power is almost entirely in abeyance, as when I have just awaked from sleep, or emerged from a swoon. But even in these states the activity of intelligence is not entirely absent; for I at least distinguish the speck of light from the surrounding darkness; I locate it with more or less accuracy; and I distinguish it from myself as a particular object. Now we have here one of the simplest forms in which the thinking subject builds up for himself an intelligible world. Without the sensitivity to light, there would be for the subject no object at all; but without the interpretative activity of thought the sensitivity would have no meaning, *i.e.* it would not be grasped as a particular phase of a single world. Perception is, therefore, not the mere presence of a particular sensation or image, but the discrimination of its elements, and the comprehension of these as involving certain fixed conditions under which they occur. If we exclude the interpretative activity of thought there is for us no object; and, therefore, no knowledge. It is only because this grasp of the particular as an instance of fixed connexion in experience is overlooked, that perception is supposed to be possible without the combined distinction and unification which is due to the activity of the thinking subject. But this activity is not the external relation of individual sensations. Sensibility as such is not an object of knowledge, but only particular sensations grasped as indicating fixed connexions in their occurrence. Hence thought is present in what is called sensation, in so far as sensation enters into our experience; and when present it interprets sensation by reference to its fixed conditions. The content of sensation does not fall without, but within thought; and it is this thought content which constitutes the world of our perception. That world is from the first a connected whole, in which every element is on the one hand referred to a single world, and on the other hand to a single subject. Nor can the one be separated from the other, for the unity of the world is made possible by the unifying activity of the subject. It must also be observed that this unifying activity is not the activity of a principle which merely operates through the individual subject: it is essentially the activity of a self-determining subject, which is conscious of a single world only in so far as in every phase of its experience it is self-active. The degree in which the world is comprehended is proportionate to the self-activity of the intelligent subject; and thus the world, while it never loses its unity, is continually growing in complexity and systematic unity. There is a single self-consistent world, because the world is a systematic unity, and because reason in all self-conscious beings is an organic unity, identical in nature, but distinct in its individual activity. Mr. Balfour assumes that the denial of a given "matter of sense" is the same thing as the denial of all determinate reality. But, in truth, the denial of the former is essential to the preservation of the latter. It is only in so far as the sensible is discriminated by thought, that there is any determinate object of knowledge; and it is only in so far as these discriminated elements are combined by the activity of a single subject, that there is any unity of experience. The thinking subject cannot have before him any object without grasping it by thought, or interpreting his immediate feelings by reference to the idea, explicit or implicit, of a connected system of reality. What Idealism maintains, therefore, is that the impossibility of having the consciousness of any object which cannot be combined with the consciousness of self is a proof that the world is a rational system. The whole process of knowledge consists in the ever more complete reduction of particulars to the unity of an organic whole; and, though it is true that a complete knowledge of the world is never attained, Idealism affirms that, were knowledge complete, the world would be found to be rational through and through. Perhaps what has been said will help to show that what Idealism denies is not that the world is concrete, but that its concreteness can be explained by any theory which starts from the fiction of an irreducible "matter of sense," *i.e.* a "matter" assumed to be absolutely opaque to a rational being.

Mr. Balfour assumes that thought deals purely with abstractions or relations, and it is on this ground that he charges Idealism with "constituting the universe out of categories." The falsity of this view has already been indicated, but the point is so important that it seems advisable to dwell upon it somewhat more fully, especially as even Mr. Bradley seems to me to have lent the weight of his authority to what I must regard as the survival of an obsolete mode of thought.

There can be no thought whatever, whether it takes the form of conception, judgment, or inference, unless thought is itself a principle of unity. This unity, however, must not be conceived as working by the method of abstraction, but as manifesting itself in the distinction and combination of differences. We can, no doubt, fix our attention upon the unity which is implied in every act of thought, but we cannot affirm that thought is a unity which excludes differences. Thought is thus the universal capacity of combining differences in a unity. Now, if thought is by its very nature a unity, there can be no absolute separation between the various elements which it combines—no separation, that is, within thought itself. It is perhaps not impossible that there are real elements which thought cannot reduce to unity, but within thought itself there can be no such elements: elements which are not combined are not thought. We cannot therefore regard the organism of thought as made up of a number of independent conceptions or ideas having no relation to one another; the whole of our conceptions taken together form the unity which thought by its activity constitutes. Conception is thus the process in which the distinguishable aspects of the real world, or what we believe to be the real world, are combined in the unity of a single system. This process may be viewed either as a progressive differentiation or as a progressive unification. And these two aspects are essentially correlative: conception reaches a higher stage according as it unites a greater number of differences, and it cannot unite without distinguishing. It is of great importance to keep hold of this truth. To neglect it is to make a consistent theory of knowledge impossible. If conception is a process of abstraction, thought can by no possibility comprehend reality. The importance of the subject will excuse a few remarks upon the nature of "conception" and its relation to judgment.

Conception may be regarded as the termination or as the beginning of a judgment, according to our point of view. In the former case conception condenses, or holds in a transparent unity, the distinguishable elements which have been combined in a prior judgment, or rather it is the synthetic unity of a number of prior judgments. Thus the conception "light" comprehends the prior judgments by which the object "light" has entered into the world of our thought. Hence it is that judgment has been supposed to be merely the analysis of a given conception. But no analysis of a conception can yield more than has previously been combined. The name "light" stands for more or fewer judgments according to the stage of thought of the individual who employs it. A so-called analytic judgment is simply the explicit statement of judgments already made, and adds nothing to the wealth of the thought-world. It is true that the resolution of a conception into the judgments which it presupposes may be the occasion of a new judgment. It is so when we for the first time observe that a conception does presuppose a number of judgments; but in this case we have done more than merely analyse the conception into its constituent elements: we have brought to light the nature of conception and its relation to judgment.

It is characteristic of every real judgment — every judgment which is more than the reproduction of a judgment formerly made — that it combines in a new unity elements not previously combined. Can we then say that judgment is the combination of conceptions? Not if we mean by this that the conceptions remain in the judgment what they were prior to the judgment. A conception being the condensed result of prior judgments in which distinguishable elements of reality have been united, it forms the starting-point for new judgments, but each of these new judgments is the further comprehension of the real, and therefore the conception grows richer in content with each judgment. Thus if, starting from the ordinary conception of "light," we go on to judge that it is "due to the vibration of an æther," we do not simply add a new predicate to the subject, but the conception is itself transformed and enriched. Judgment is thus conception viewed as in process, and a conception is any stage in that process. The distinction is purely relative. In judgment thought unifies the elements which it discriminates; in conception the elements are viewed as united even while they are discriminated. For it must be observed that thought never unifies without discriminating: the whole process of thought is concrete throughout, and, as knowledge develops, becomes more and more concrete. We are therefore entitled to say that for the thinking subject reality is in continual process, and we are also entitled to say that there is neither thinking subject nor thought reality outside of the process of thought. A real world which is not capable of being thought is for the subject nothing, and a subject which is not capable of thinking the real world is also nothing.

If this view is correct, it is misleading to say, with Mr. Bradley, that "in judgment an idea is predicated of a reality."* For the reality of which we judge is a reality which exists only for thought, and it has no content except that which it has received in the process by which it is constituted for thought. Mr. Bradley tells us that whatever we regard as real has two aspects, (*a*) existence, (*b*) content, and that "thought seems essentially to consist in their division." Now, it is no doubt true that, if we suppose the real to be something which exists apart from thought, we shall have to divide or separate the "what"

* *Appearance and Reality*, p. 163.

from the "that." But there is for us no real in addition to the real which is thought. Such a real is a pure abstraction, and means no more than the empty possibility of the real. We cannot separate in this hypothetical real between the "that" and the "what," because, having no content, it is neither a "that" nor a "what." The real only comes to be for us in so far as there has gone on a process of discrimination and unification within a single reality, by means of which the real has been constituted as a thought or ideal reality. What Mr. Bradley calls the "that" seems to me merely a name for the unity which is involved in every phase of the process by which reality is thought; and what he calls the "what" is a name for the elements which thought distinguishes and combines in the unity of the real. The "that" has therefore no determinateness when it is separated from the "what"; it is simply pure being, or the bare potentiality of a thought reality. Mr. Bradley allows himself to speak of the "what" as if it were first "presented" in unity with the "that," and of judgment as if it consisted in the "division" of the "what" from the "that." But surely there is no "what" except that which thought has already made its own. The subject of any judgment has already a content, it is true, and this content we may express in the form of a series of judgments; but these judgments will merely reproduce the judgments formerly made: they will add nothing to knowledge. Every new judgment, on the other hand, *determines* the conceived reality from which we start: it transforms the reality for thought, and thus enriches it by a new determination. There would be no reason for judging at all if judgment merely consisted in detaching a "content" from "existence," and then proceeding to attach it to "existence." The "existence" and the "content" are one and indivisible, and as the one grows, so also does the other. Mr. Bradley says that "an idea implies the separation of content from existence." And no doubt in every judgment the "content" is held suspended in thought before it is predicated of the subject. But, in the first place, so long as it is so held, there is no judgment: judgment consists in determining the subject *by* the predicate. And, in the second place, the content which is thus predicated of the subject is not the content which is already involved in the subject, and therefore we cannot say that judgment consists in the separation of the " what " from the " that." When the scientific man affirms that light is due to the vibration of an æther, he does not separate the " content " already involved in the conception of the luminous object, and then predicate this " content " of the subject; what he does is to determine the already qualified subject by a totally new " content " which it did not previously possess, and in this determination of the subject the judgment consists. It thus seems to me that Mr. Bradley gives countenance to two fallacies; first, that the subject is a mere " that " instead of being the condensed result of the whole prior process of thought; and, secondly, that judgment consists in the separation of a given content from the " that," a content which is then attributed to the " that "; whereas judgment consists in the predication of a *new* content, which develops and enriches the " that." Whatever difficulty attaches to this view arises, as it seems to me, from the assumption that reality exists apart from the process by which it is thought. And no doubt reality is not made by thought in the sense of being the creation of the individual thinking subject, but it is made for the subject in the sense that nothing is or can be real for him which is not revealed to him in the process by which he thinks it as real.

When Mr. Bradley says that "the subject has unspecified content which is not stated in the predicate" (168), he is evidently confusing "the subject" with reality, as it would be could it be completely determined by thought. But such a subject is not the "that" which is distinguished from the "what," for the "that" is merely the abstraction of reality,—the abstract idea of reality in general which is no reality in particular. Such a subject has no "unspecified content," because it has no content whatever. But if by the "subject" is meant the complete system of reality, it is no doubt true that it has "unspecified content which is not stated in the predicate." No single judgment can express the infinite wealth of the totality of reality. And not only is this true, but no single judgment can express the wealth of reality even as it exists for the subject who frames the judgment. We can only express the nature of reality in the totality of judgments which express the nature of reality as known to us, and it is manifestly an inadequate or partial view which seeks to limit known reality to that aspect of it which is expressed in a single judgment. But we must go still further; not only is known reality not expressed in any single judgment, but it is not expressed in the whole system of judgments which embody the knowledge of man as it exists at any given time. Our knowledge is not complete, and I do not see how it ever can be complete. In that sense reality or the absolute must always be unknown. But unless reality in its true nature is different in kind from the reality which we know, it must be thinkable reality. Any other reality than that which is thinkable can have no community with thought reality, but must be absolutely unknowable. It is not maintained that there is no reality which is not thought by us, but only that the reality which we know is thought reality. This reality enters into our thought and forms its content, and as the content continually expands for us, so the reality continually expands. Reflecting upon this characteristic of knowledge, we get the notion of a completely determined reality, a reality which would be present to thought if thought were absolutely complete. Such a reality we do not possess, and it is therefore natural to say that there is a defect in the character of our thought which prevents us from grasping reality in its completeness. This explanation seems to me to rest upon the assumption that reality cannot be thought because thought deals only with abstractions. But, as I have maintained above, thought is never abstract; it contains within itself the whole wealth of reality, so far as reality is known to us. The defect is not in the character of thought, as distinguished from feeling or intuition, but in the very nature of man as a being in whom knowledge is a never-ending process. What I contend for, then, is not that man has complete knowledge of reality, — a contention which is manifestly absurd, — but that reality in its completeness must be a thinkable reality. Any other view seems to me to lead to the *caput mortuum* of the thing-in-itself, the reality which cannot be thought because it is unthinkable. When, therefore, Mr. Bradley says that it is an untenable position to maintain that "in reality there is nothing beyond what is made thought's object" (169), I agree with a *caveat*. That there is nothing which is not made "thought's object" is manifestly untrue, if the "thought" here spoken of is thought as it exists for man. But, if it is meant that there is in reality something which cannot be made the object of thought, because it is unthinkable, I do not see what sort of reality this can be; to me it seems to be merely a name for a metaphysical abstraction. Reality that *cannot* be thought is a sort of reality to which I find myself unable to attach any meaning, and until I find some one who can give a meaning to it, I refuse to admit its possibility. But I feel certain that such a person cannot be found, for the obvious reason that if this supposititious reality had a meaning, it would no longer be unthinkable.

If these considerations are at all correct, the only reality which has any meaning for us is reality that is capable of being thought. And this reality is not for us stationary, but grows in content as thought, which is the faculty of unifying the distinguishable elements of reality, develops in the process by which those elements are more fully distinguished and unified. The reality which thus enters into and constitutes our thought is therefore not abstract but infinitely concrete. For, as we have seen, the process of thought is not the mere transition from one conception to another, but it is the internal development of conception, which is at the same time the development of the conceived world. The reality, therefore, which thus arises for us in the process of thought is a system, in which there is revealed an ever greater diversity brought back into an ever more complete unity. And this reality is the absolute, so far as the absolute enters into and constitutes our known world. To seek for the absolute beyond the thought reality, which alone exists for us, is to seek the living among the dead; if the absolute is not revealed to us in the reality that we know, it is for us nothing.

CHAPTER VII

IDEALISM IN RELATION TO AGNOSTICISM AND THE SPECIAL SCIENCES

I. AGNOSTICISM

In the preceding chapter an attempt has been made to explain and defend the general doctrine of Idealism, which affirms that the knowable world is identical with the world as it really is, and is a systematic or rational unity. This doctrine is of course diametrically opposed to Agnosticism. In a former work* it was maintained that Agnosticism is a self-contradictory theory, because in affirming an absolute limit to human knowledge, it assumes the knowledge of a realm of reality distinct from the realm of phenomena, and tacitly affirms that there are two kinds of intelligence, corresponding to these two realms. Two objections have been raised which it may

* *Comte, Mill, and Spencer*, Chap. II.

be well to consider. It is objected, firstly, that my criticism applies only to a dogmatic affirmation or denial of a noumenal reality; and, secondly, that even if such a reality is admitted, it is not a legitimate inference that its advocates are bound in consistency to assume two kinds of intelligence.

(1) As to the first point, it must be answered, that a purely sceptical attitude is impossible. Such an attitude would mean, presumably, that he who assumes it refuses to say whether there is any reality other than that which is known by us: there may, or may not, be such a reality, but we are not in a position to give any answer either positive or negative. Now, it is hard to see how any one can affirm that we are unable to say whether that which we call reality is or is not reality, without basing his affirmation upon some limitation in the nature of our faculty of knowledge. Surely the inability on our part to determine whether we have any knowledge of reality or not, implies that our faculty of knowledge is by its very nature unable to distinguish between truth and false-

hood. But if we cannot distinguish between truth and falsehood, no proposition whatever can be held by us to be either true or false; and therefore our affirmation that we cannot distinguish between truth or falsehood cannot be accepted as true. If it is not true, there is no affirmation whatever, but only the delusive appearance of affirmation; and to such a delusive appearance we can attach no meaning; it may be either the affirmation or denial of reality or some *tertium quid;* it is, in fact, that logical monster, an affirmative-negative proposition. In short, if you make any judgment whatever which means anything, you have assumed the reality of your judgment, though not of what you affirm or deny in your judgment; and thus you have assumed that so far at least you have touched solid reality. A purely sceptical attitude is thus a contradiction in terms,— an affirmation which affirms nothing, or a denial which denies nothing. The most complete sceptic that ever lived assumed that his scepticism was real, and to that extent he was a dogmatist.

(2) It is further maintained that even if the distinction between the phenomenal and the real is admitted, it does not follow that there must be two kinds of intelligence corresponding to these two realms. After what has been said, it must be obvious that this objection is unsound. For, if our intelligence is not capable of knowing reality, it must be because of an absolute limit in the character of our intelligence, and if that limit were removed reality, admitting it to exist, would be capable of being grasped by us. Now, the dogmatic phenomenalist, and even, as has been shown, the so-called sceptical phenomenalist, assumes that there is reality. No western thinker, so far as I know, has had the courage to affirm that there is no reality whatever: that sublime height has been reached only in the east. Now, if there is reality at all, it must be comprehensible by some intelligence. It may be said that there is no such intelligence, or at least that we cannot know that there is such an intelligence. But surely we are entitled to demand that no affirmation should be made

which is meaningless. The phenomenalist, then, admits that there is reality, and in so doing he assumes that he is saying something which has a meaning for himself, and for others who hear or read what he says. Now what is a reality which is not a reality for some intelligence? Make any predication you like about it, and you will find that, if you mean anything at all, you mean that it is present to an intelligence. If you refuse to make any predication about it, it is not reality but pure nothingness. Hence you cannot say: "There is reality," without assuming that reality has a meaning, and to say that it has a meaning is to say that it is relative to some intelligence. Now the phenomenalist affirms that reality is not the object of *his* intelligence, and therefore it must be the object of some other intelligence, or it is nothing at all. And this other intelligence cannot involve an absolute limit, as our intelligence is assumed to do, because if it did it would not grasp reality but only appearance; in other words, the phenomenalist in affirming the absolute limitation of his own intelligence has tacitly assumed an intelligence free from limits. I was therefore right in saying that from the doctrine of the relativity of knowledge it is a legitimate inference that there are two kinds of intelligence, one absolutely limited and the other absolutely unlimited. The absurdity of this doctrine I shall not again insist upon: I shall only repeat that an intelligence which is absolutely limited would never know that it was absolutely limited, since in that case it would be beyond the assumed limits.

Now if it is admitted that there is a rational or intelligible system of things, it is obvious that with this single system all the sciences must deal. Reality is one, and to suppose it split up into bits by the concentration of attention upon one phase of it, is to be the victim of an abstraction. When in geometry we define a point or line, we are not dealing with a "mere idea," but with a fixed relation holding for every subject for whom there is any reality whatever. Similarly, all the judgments of geometry imply that there are unchanging relations in the one system of reality which alone is or can be known, and these unchanging relations constitute the objectivity of that system, so far as it comes within the view of geometry. This does not mean that there is a world constituted of nothing but geometrical relations, but it does mean that a world from which all geometrical relations are eliminated is unthinkable. If geometrical relations are not determinations of the real world, all the sciences of nature are made impossible, and, as a consequence, the whole of the philosophical sciences as well. What is said of spatial relations, of course, holds good also of temporal relations. And when we pass from the mathematical determination of reality to the dynamical—from space and time to matter and motion—the same principle of explanation still applies. For dynamical relations are real aspects of the one system of reality, while yet they do not exhaust its nature. It is as great a mistake to deny that those relations are determinations of the absolute as to affirm that in them we have reached an exhaustive definition of it. A world of matter and motion is real in the same sense that a world of space or a world of time is real; *without* dynamical relations there could be no reality whatever, but a reality consisting of these relations *alone* — a world of pure matter and motion — is as impossible as a world of pure space or pure time. They are real, unchangeable aspects of existence, but they are no more than aspects. For, though there would be no real world were the relations or laws of dynamics not unchangeable, there are other aspects of reality which still further define existence. Certain of these aspects are brought to light by physics, chemistry, and biology. Here again we may say that what the sciences affirm they affirm of the absolute, but we cannot say that now at last we have reached the ultimate or complete determination of it. All the sciences, from mathematics to biology inclusive, are abstract in this sense, that there are other aspects of reality which they presuppose. These new aspects of the one single system of reality form the subject-matter of the philosophical sciences, which again presuppose logic or metaphysic as the science which deals directly with the interrelation of all the principles upon which the other sciences are based.

II. MATHEMATICS

The view which has just been indicated implies that mathematics is a science, *i.e.* contains propositions which are true or hold of reality. These propositions are, as I believe, true formulations of fundamental conditions or relations by which the real world is characterised, though they are certainly not a formulation of *all* those conditions. What is held is not that mathematics formulates "the intellectual conditions of sensible reality," if this means that there is an absolute separation between "sensible reality" and another reality which may be defined as non-sensible. There are not two realities, but only one. What is called "sensible reality" is either the fiction of a world supposed to be given in immediate sensation, or it is a term for certain aspects of the one reality, the only reality there is. To speak of "sensible reality" as contrasted with non-sensible or supersensible reality is to fall back into that untenable phenomenalism, the contradictory character of which has already been maintained. Mathematics, then, concentrates its attention upon certain very simple conditions or relations of the one and only reality, and, as I believe, is successful in formulating their nature.

It may be objected, however, that this view of mathematics takes no account of the recent doctrine that Euclidean geometry merely states the conditions of our space of three dimensions. Now it might fairly be answered that it is incumbent upon the advocates of imaginary geometry to reconcile their doctrine with any tenable theory of knowledge. Does their hypothetical space of four or more dimensions *contradict* our space of three dimensions? If it does, they deny the principle of contradiction, contradict themselves, and can prove neither the reality of a space of four nor a space of three dimensions, since they cannot prove the reality of any space whatever, or of anything else. It seems advisable, however, to deal more directly with the question. The discussion will necessarily be brief, but I shall try to indicate the main points. Let me repeat that I do not for a moment deny the value of imaginary geometry as a system of mathematical symbols. I should as soon think of denying the value of the Cartesian co-ordinates. What I deny is the *philosophical* doctrine based upon the symbolic constructions of mathematics, — the doctrine that a space of four or more dimensions is a possible reality. I must also warn the reader that I cannot deal with the mutually discrepant philosophical views of those who argue for the phenomenality of our space of three dimensions. I shall further limit myself mainly to Riemann and Helmholtz. I may mention, however, that I find the conclusions which I reached several years ago endorsed by such eminent logicians as Sigwart and Wundt, not to speak of Lotze.

(1) I find Riemann, then, arguing in this way: Space is a logical species of which the logical genus is extended magnitude or mul-

tiplicity (*Mannigfaltigkeit*); hence, though our space is the only one of which we have actual experience, it is not the only possible space. If it is objected that Riemann is "antiquated," let me cite Bruno Erdmann. I have not read Erdmann's treatise, having ceased to take any interest in the question after my study of Riemann and Helmholtz, but I quote the statement of his view from Wundt's *Logik* (I. 440). His view is, then, that "modern geometry has been able to find a more general conception, under which space may be subsumed as a particular species, and from which therefore by the introduction of determinate conditions the fundamental properties of space may be developed analytically." Now I have no hesitation in saying that this supposed subsumption of space under a logical genus is a blunder, which the best modern logicians have clearly exposed. The whole idea of determining the real relations of things by the formation of an ascending series of abstractions is utterly untenable, resting as it does upon the mediæval idea of logic as a purely formal science. The real world as it exists for our conceptual thought is not obtained by abstraction from full-formed individuals given in perception, but by a concrete process in which the first immediate judgments of perception are transformed by the comprehension of the fundamental relations, implied in those judgments, and brought to light in the complex process in which knowledge is developed. To run up and down a logical "Porphyry's tree" is a travesty of the process of thought, which corresponds to nothing "in heaven above, or the earth beneath, or the waters under the earth." But, even if we grant that the subsumption of logical species under a genus is a valid process, it would not prove that our space is only one of several possible species of space. For the whole account of the formation of logical species rests upon the presupposition that the ultimate datum from which we start is the individual. Now the individual in this case is our three-dimensional space, and hence we cannot reason from the general conception of extended magnitude to the possible reality of several *species* of space. We can get nothing out of the conception of extended magnitude but what we have put into it; hence, when we descend the logical tree which we have previously ascended, we shall find at the end just what we had at the beginning, and what we had at the beginning was an individual space of three dimensions. Riemann so far admits this as to say that our space of three dimensions rests upon "experience," but he still supposes that conception is wider than "experience," and hence that there is nothing to hinder us from supposing a space of four or more dimensions. There is, of course, nothing to hinder us from *thinking* of a space of four or more dimensions, but the possible *reality* of such a space cannot be deduced from the abstract conception of extended magnitude. That conception is limited by what is already contained under it, and there is only one space contained under it, not several species of space. I hold, then, that in reasoning from logical genus to logical species, Riemann has fallen into the logical mistake of supposing that possible reality can be determined by logical possibility. In support of what I have said let me quote a few sentences from Wundt. Referring to Erdmann, he says: "This view must at least be so far corrected, that the question cannot be in regard to a relation of genus and species in the ordinary logical sense. If a genus is to be formed, several species must be given which possess certain common marks. But in this case only *one* space is given to our perception." And then he goes on to point out that "we can never possess an actual image of spaces different from ours." "An opposite view," he continues, "seems to be maintained by some mathematicians, who hold that we can make a sensible picture of spaces of another kind, as *e.g.* a space which consists merely of a plane or of a spherical or pseudo-spherical surface."* This brings us to what I regard as another fallacy of those who maintain the possible reality of a space other than ours.

(2) Helmholtz seeks to commend his view that a space other than ours can not only be thought but presented to the imagination, by the fiction of beings living in a plane, or a sphere, and limited in their consciousness to

* Wundt's *Logik:* I. 440-1.

the plane or the sphere. The whole supposition seems to me absurd and self-contradictory. There is no difficulty whatever in thinking of beings limited to a plane or sphere; for such beings are to all intents and purposes identical with the plane or sphere; but what we cannot do is to think of their *consciousness* as superficial or spherical. A superficial or spherical consciousness has no meaning whatever that I can discover. Now, if our supposititious beings have not a superficial or spherical consciousness, we must suppose that the plane or the sphere is an object which they can think and reason about. But, if they have before their consciousness only a plane or a sphere, they will not have any geometry such as we possess, because a plane is the boundary of a solid, and a curve is relative to a tangent. Such beings would therefore have no geometry whatever. This seems obvious if we carry out Helmholtz's suggestion, and suppose beings limited to a *point*. Will any one affirm that a point has any meaning except as the boundary of a line? In short, a plane or sphere is intelligible only because it is a figure in our three-dimensional space. To reason from the curvature of a plane or sphere to the curvature of space seems to me a palpable fallacy. Space has no curvature, though figures in space have. Let me again support my view by a quotation from Wundt. "When we deal with the geometry of the plane," says Wundt, "our spatial idea is no other than in the geometry of space; we merely leave out of consideration all spatial relations except the plane; we do the same in the investigation of the geometrical properties of spherical or pseudo-spherical surfaces. Those relations of space from which we thus abstract have no existence apart from our idea; on the contrary, we require our complete space-perception, not only for the idea of a curved surface, but even for the idea of a surface or a line, for we can no more imagine the surface than the line except as in space: we imagine both not as independent spaces, but as figures in space."*

(3) It is supposed that because functions of magnitude can be converted into geometrical relations of a thinkable space, there may be

* Ibid. I. 441.

beings who enjoy the consciousness of a space of n dimensions. Surely this is an untenable inference. We can think of systems in which four, five, or any number of elements are required, instead of the three elements which space demands for the determination of the position of a point. But, in order to give a geometrical meaning to analytical operations, we have to refer to our space of three dimensions. "It is self-evident," says Wundt, "that mathematical speculations, which infer that our space must be related to a four-dimensional magnitude in the same way as the surface is related to our space, cannot of themselves be the basis for the imaginability of a space of four or more dimensions. This question stands upon precisely the same level as that with which the older ontology occupied itself, viz. whether the actual world is or is not the best of all possible worlds."* I will conclude with a passage from Sigwart. "The result of these enquiries," says Sigwart, "is not that it is left to experience to decide whether we are to assume the plane space of Euclid, or a

* Ibid. I. 443.

space which is in some way curved; but only that from the purely logical standpoint of analysis the quantitative relations of space are not to be derived as the necessary form of a manifold which varies in three directions, but that on the contrary they are actual, because based upon an unanalysable necessity of our space-perception, which is essentially different from any law which can be expressed in numbers and numerical relations. They open up no possibility of extending our space-perception, or of representing a non-Euclidian geometry not merely in analytical formulæ, but also for actual perception; we remain subject to those laws of space according to which we first think of it, and it is as certain that Euclid will remain unrefuted in geometry, as it is that Aristotle in his principle of contradiction has outlived the Hegelian logic." *

III. THE PHYSICAL SCIENCES

I conclude, then, that there is nothing in the speculations of "pangeometry" to support

* Sigwart's *Logic*. English tr., II. 566.

the view of phenomenalists either that our consciousness has certain forms of perception peculiar to itself, as Helmholtz maintains, or as others hold that there may be an external world which lies in a space of four or more dimensions. To set forth all the objections which beset these views would be to write a whole system of philosophy, but I hope I have at least succeeded in indicating some of them. The world of the mathematician is, however, very far from being reality in its completeness; it exists only as the construction of the mathematician, though that construction rests upon unchangeable relations or conditions of the one reality which alone exists. Hence, when we pass to the physical sciences we have made a considerable advance in the determination of those relations or conditions. There are, however, two fundamental mistakes which we must here seek to avoid: the mistake of supposing that science merely "describes" the world of sensible perception, as Kirchhoff seems to say, and the mistake of imagining that the laws of science are more than an abstract or partial determination of reality. The theory of knowledge which many scientific men advance, when they leave their proper task and assume the rôle of the logician, is usually a curious mixture of these opposite errors.

Our first view of the world naturally is that things lie before us in perception, and that, in order to know them, we must take them as they present themselves, carefully excluding all preconceptions, and accurately observing their qualities and determining the quantity of each quality. Without observation of this kind there can be no science of nature, but it can hardly be said yet to be science; or, at least, it can be called science only when the observer is guided in his selection of facts by ideas of relation. What underlies scientific observation is a faith in the presence in nature of conditions or relations which remain permanent under all the changes of particulars. It must be observed, therefore, that science transforms the ordinary view of the world by penetrating to those permanent conditions or relations which are not obvious to perception, but are only brought to light by the persistent endeavour to find the identical in the different. The reality which science discovers is in one way an ideal world, a world which exists only as a construction of the scientific intellect, but it is at the same time a much truer apprehension of reality than that ordinary view of things from which science is developed, though it may be said that the ordinary view contains implicitly more than science does justice to. Thus the physicist and chemist virtually set aside all the sensible relations of things, — not because these fall outside of the real world, but because they do not come within the scope of their science, — leaving them to be dealt with by the more concrete sciences of physiology and psychology. If, therefore, we fail to observe the transformation which science effects in our ordinary view of the world, we shall fall into the mistake of supposing that it is merely a "description" of sensible objects, and if we insist upon the reality of the abstract world of relations upon which science, for its own purposes, concentrates attention, we shall fall into the opposite mistake of hypostatising this abstract world, and identifying it with the real world in its completeness. These two defects are closely related to each other; for it is just because we overlook the partial or abstract character of the laws of science that we convert relations into vague and shadowy *things;* and it is because we do not see that science adopts a negative attitude towards immediate perception that we suppose it to leave sensible reality as it was before scientific insight has broken it up, and are led to regard laws of nature as a refined transcript of the sensible, instead of being, what they are, a purely conceptual world of fixed conditions and relations, implied no doubt in the world of ordinary observation, but not brought into clear consciousness and made an object of direct consideration. Thus Comte tells us that science confines itself to the investigation of the laws of the resemblance, coexistence, and succession of phenomena, and he assumes that these laws are simply the generalised restatement or description of the phenomena themselves. But a law is something more than a generalised restatement or description of phenomena, if by "phenomena" we mean the objects of ordinary observation. For a law is contrasted with phenomena as the permanent relation in the changing particular, as that which is identical in spite of all differences, as the principle by reference to which particulars are seen to be more than mere phenomena or transitory phases of reality. Were it not possible to penetrate to such permanent, identical, or unchanging relations, we should have no science of nature. It is nothing to the point that no law is final, for the development of science, like all other developments, consists in an ever fuller comprehension of fixed relations, or what are usually called "uniformities," a development which does not simply set aside the relations already discovered, but combines them in a higher synthesis; indeed, if this were not the case, science would at every fresh advance throw down all that it had laboriously built up and start *de novo*.

Now, if we keep in mind these two aspects

of a scientific law,—that it is, on the one hand, the revelation of a principle which is established only by a necessary but in a sense an artificial simplification of reality, and that this principle is, after all, only a permanent relation of the changing,—we shall, I think, be led to see that a law of nature, as it is not a "description" of phenomena, so it is not a description of "uniformities." A "uniformity," if we are to give the word anything like its ordinary meaning, is naturally regarded as a customary or frequent repetition of a given resemblance, sequence, or coexistence; and it is in this sense that Mill and many scientific men who make an incursion into the field of logic are disposed to interpret a law. It was in contrast to this doctrine that I ventured to challenge Mill's view of induction as based upon "resemblance," instead of "identity."* The "identity," of course, as any one who reads what I have said with ordinary care will see, is not that of a changeless "substance" or "thing,"—I do not admit the reality of such fictions at all,—but of a relation. No two

* *Comte, Mill, and Spencer*, pp. 92-3.

individuals are alike; but in all their differences they may agree in a certain feature, and this agreement is the basis of induction.

Now, when we ask what bearing this view of a law of nature has upon the question of the relativity of knowledge, it is no answer to say that science is entirely neutral. In one way that is a bare tautology. Science as such is not a theory of knowledge; and, of course, having no theory of knowledge, it does not tell us what the ultimate nature of reality is; but the question is whether the view of reality, which in the pursuit of his special object the scientific man naturally adopts, can be regarded as ultimate. The attempt to answer this question leads us into the region of philosophy, and compels us to ask what is the general view of reality upon which science is based; and the answer, as we may be certain, cannot fail to be coloured by the general theory of knowledge which commends itself to those who seek to answer the question. A phenomenalist theory of knowledge will find support in science for its doctrine, because it will interpret scientific conclusions from that point of view, and so in other cases. I have tried to explain why I cannot accept the phenomenalist interpretation. I cannot accept it, because, as it seems to me, it does not do justice to the real advance beyond ordinary observation which science makes, and because it does not take due note of the abstract or partial character of the scientific view of reality. On this last point I should like to say a word or two.

We are too apt to talk glibly of "laws of nature" or "uniformities of nature," not seeing that two discrepant views of reality are concealed beneath this ambiguous phraseology. Is "nature" simply a term for an aggregate of phenomena? or is it a real unity or organic system? Mill tells us that we cannot properly speak of the "uniformity" of nature, but only of "uniformities" of nature. Now, waiving the objection I have already made that science deals with identities and not with uniformities, and interpreting the term "uniformity" in its higher sense, it is obvious that to deny any identity or unity in nature is to deny that reality is an organic system. But this is the same as saying that all we can know of reality is that in point of fact we find certain relations which, so far as our experience goes, have not changed, but which, for aught we can show, might change at any moment. Thus, under the denial of the uniformity or unity of nature, Mill and others assume the phenomenalist view of knowable reality; and when they are asked to substantiate their assumption, they fall back upon a sensationalist theory of knowledge, and a metaphysical theory of the absolute limitation of our knowledge to phenomena. To one who rejects the sensationalist epistemology and is convinced of the self-contradictory character of the phenomenalist metaphysic, the denial of the systematic unity of the real seems a denial of all knowledge and of all reality. I content myself with pointing out this result of the ordinary view of laws of nature as implying nothing but observed uniformities, having already dwelt sufficiently upon what I regard as the defects of sensationalism and phenomenalism. To me it seems to be one of the gifts which a true philosophy conveys, to bring to light that organic unity of nature which is implicit in science. For "nature" has no meaning apart from a unifying intelligence, and to deny the unity of nature is to deny the unity of intelligence and to make all knowledge impossible. I admit, however, or rather contend, that the organic unity of reality lies beyond the horizon of the specialist in physics, and even in chemistry; but the biologist, from the character of the objects with which he deals, is almost invariably more readily disposed to hold that the real world is an organic unity. In proof of this it is enough to refer to Darwin himself, whose whole doctrine is inspired by the idea of such a unity, though he fails to give a philosophical formulation of it; and to the recent developments of biology, which have been more and more in this direction.

IV. BIOLOGY

The doctrine of natural selection, while it compels us to abandon the external or mechanical idea of teleology associated with the name of Paley, is incompetent to explain knowledge or morality. To this view it has been objected that the doctrine of evolution, as held by Darwin and many of his followers, cannot be identified with the doctrine of natural selection, and that I have therefore confused true Darwinism with the views of Wallace and Weissmann. This objection does not seem to me to affect in any way the point which I sought to establish. My aim was to show that, without assuming anything but what is admitted by all biologists, a certain philosophical conclusion, not contemplated or even denied by certain biologists, must yet be reached. That conclusion was that an immanent teleology may be legitimately deduced from the doctrine of natural selection. It was not necessary for my purpose to embroil myself in the questions at issue between Wallace, Weissmann, and others, while by doing so I should have given occasion for the retort that teleology has nothing to do with the biological doctrine of evolutionary descent. That this is no fanciful danger may be shown by a single extract from Huxley's account of the reception of the

Origin of Species in Darwin's *Life and Letters*. "Having got rid," says Huxley, "of the belief in chance and the disbelief in design, *as in no sense appurtenances of evolution*, the third libel upon that doctrine, that it is anti-theistic, might perhaps be left to shift for itself. . . . The doctrine of evolution does not even come into contact with theism, considered as a philosophical doctrine."* To this view I entirely assent; but, as it seems to me, we may, accepting the scientific doctrine of evolutionary descent, go on to base upon it a philosophical argument in favour of a teleological view of the world. It may be said, however, that it is illegitimate to speak of Darwinism as synonymous with the doctrine of natural selection. And no doubt it is true that, in the wider sense of the term, the biological doctrine of evolution, as held by Darwin, admitted other factors than natural selection; but it will be admitted that the great achievement of Darwin was the destruction of the old rigid separation of species by the theory of natural selection. This was all

* Darwin's *Life and Letters:* Am. ed., I. 555-6.

that I contended, and all that my argument required me to deal with. In taking this view I might have supported myself by the authority of Huxley. In the essay already quoted, that eminent biologist says: "The suggestion that new species may result from the selective action of external conditions upon the variations from their specific type which individuals present . . . is the central idea of the *Origin of Species* and *contains the quintessence of Darwinism.*" * And again, a few pages further on: "Whatever may be the ultimate fate of the particular theory put forth by Darwin [the "particular theory," as the context shows, being natural selection], I venture to affirm that, so far as my knowledge goes, all the ingenuity and all the learning of hostile critics has not enabled them to adduce a solitary fact, of which it can be said this is irreconcilable with the Darwinian theory." † Here Huxley tells us that natural selection is "the quintessence of Darwinism," and that opponents have not adduced "a solitary fact, of which it can be said this is irrecon-

* Ibid. I. 548-9.   † Ibid. I. 552.

cilable with the Darwinian theory," meaning the theory of natural selection. Surely what Huxley here means is that what was *distinctive* of Darwin was the doctrine of natural selection. It seems unnecessary to dwell further upon this point, but it may be worth while, for other reasons, to cite a few of Darwin's own expressions. To begin with, what did Darwin call his first great book? He called it *The Origin of Species by Means of Natural Selection.* In the autobiography he says: "The old argument from design in nature, as given by Paley, which formerly seemed to me so conclusive, fails, *now that the law of natural selection has been discovered.* . . . There seems to be no more design in the variability of organic beings, and in the action of natural selection, than in the course which 'the wind blows."* This passage leaves no doubt whatever that in Darwin's own mind his theory was incompatible with teleology. On another occasion Darwin writes: "It is not that designed variation makes, as it seems to me, my deity

* Ibid. I. 278–9.

'natural selection' superfluous, but from seeing what an enormous field of undesigned variability there is ready for natural selection to appropriate." Now I have no desire to narrow Darwin's theory more than he narrowed it himself. I know that Darwin, with his large candour and what may be called his unconscious idealism, follows the facts wherever they lead him, and suggests modifications of his doctrine which, as he says on one occasion, "lessen the glory of natural selection"; but I think no one can deny that he always and consistently rejected teleology, and rejected it mainly "now that the law of natural selection has been discovered." Now, my argument was, rightly or wrongly, that the law of natural selection itself, when we see all its *philosophical*—not its *scientific*—implications, compels us to affirm an immanent teleology, and that it is from not taking note of these implications that Darwin himself and many of his followers suppose that knowledge and morality may be explained by the method of science. It therefore seems to me that science does not establish teleology, but that a comprehensive view of living beings, and much more of man, does establish teleology. But, after all, it is mainly a question of definition whether we call a theory scientific or philosophical; and I am quite contented to rest my case on the broad view that Darwin and many of his followers are wrong in denying teleology, though they are perfectly right in denying that mechanical form of teleology which is associated with the name of Paley.

It is important to observe that a teleological view of the world does not exclude but presupposes the law of natural causation. We must therefore be careful to avoid regarding "purpose" as a sort of *deus ex machina*, which is to be invoked when the ordinary scientific explanation has not yet been discovered. Such a conception of "purpose" in nature seems to me a survival of the obsolete idea of external teleology, from which the doctrine of development has helped to free us. I have no belief in a teleology which does not presuppose the inviolability of the natural law of causation. If a break could be found in that law, we should have to fall back upon the idea that there is no system of nature, but merely a partial and imperfect arrangement of parts. The teleology which is here maintained is based upon the recognition of a fixed order in nature. What is held is, that living beings by their very nature contain in them a principle of unity which is realised within the inviolable system of natural law.

The theory of natural selection assumes, firstly, that the laws of nature are inviolable. This is at bottom another way of saying that, when we come to the study of nature, we presuppose that it is a system of facts, so perfect that there is no break or flaw in it. Hence living beings, as well as inorganic things, are within this system, and there can be no such dissolution of continuity as that which is suggested by the view of purpose as external or mechanical. Secondly, natural selection assumes that in each living being there is a tendency or impulse to maintain itself and to continue the species. In saying that the doctrine of natural selection rests on this assumption, it is not meant that the biologist need be aware of it, or that he employs it in his specific enquiries. The specialist is hardly ever aware of the preconceptions from which he starts. What is maintained is, that reflection upon the theory of natural selection compels us to take this view. It has been said that the impulse to self-maintenance is "something wholly conditioned upon and resident within the material nature of the organism." What is to be understood by the "material nature of the organism"? Is it meant that the craving for food, for example, can be attributed to "the material nature of the organism"? If so, that impulse must be capable of being expressed in terms of matter and motion. This seems to me a mere confusion of thought, resting upon a physical metaphor which conceals the characteristic fact that sensibility does not belong to the "material nature of the organism," but is the differentia of a certain class of living beings.

Thirdly, if there were no adaptation whatever between organisms and their environment, it would be impossible for them to exist at all. It is objected that there is also harmony between "a piece of ice and the water in which it floats." No doubt; but the kind of harmony to which I refer, as is implied by the two preceding characteristics, is one which exists only in a being which is internally purposive, and that cannot be said of the piece of ice. It is no doubt true that when we have discovered that living beings are purposive, we can no longer speak of nature as if it were merely a mechanical system; but, as Kant points out, it is living beings which first clearly suggest to us that nature is purposive. And if it is true, as I have maintained, that we cannot differentiate living from non-living beings without applying the idea of purpose, we are entitled to say that reality as a whole must be interpreted from the new point of view of an immanent teleology. It is only by an artificial truncation of reality, such as is a necessary device in the pursuit of the physical sciences, that we are led to suppose that nature is merely a mechanical system. The peculiar phenomena of living beings compel us to revise our first inadequate view, and to say that real existence is not merely a mechanical but a teleological system. Having gone so far, we can hardly refuse to take the last step, and admit that the existence of self-conscious beings again compels us to revise our view of reality, and to admit that the only completely satisfactory explanation of it is that which refers the world to a self-conscious, rational, and spiritual principle.

CHAPTER VIII

IDEALISM AND CHRISTIANITY

THE conclusion to which we have been brought is that the ultimate conception by means of which existence must be explained is that of a self-conscious and self-determining principle. Now it is important to see precisely what is involved in this conception, and to remove from it all elements which are inconsistent with its purity and with the position assigned to it as the only adequate explanation of the world as a whole. A thorough discussion of this topic would demand a complete system of metaphysic, but it may be possible in brief compass to show the inadequacy of certain definitions of God or the absolute, and to indicate the definition which it would be the task of a completely reasoned system to establish. When this has been done, an attempt will be made to give an outline of the relation of the world, and especially of man, to the absolute. A consideration of these two questions will of itself be sufficient to show that Idealism is in essential harmony with the Christian ideal of life, as held by the Founder of Christianity, however it may differ, at least in form, from popular Christian theology.

(1) The absolute is very inadequately conceived when it is defined simply as substance. This view is the inevitable result of opposing mind and nature, or thought and reality, to each other as abstract opposites. For, if mind excludes nature and nature mind, we are compelled to seek for the unity of both in that which is neither, but is something beyond both. This "something," however, cannot be further defined, and hence it remains for knowledge absolutely indeterminate. Now it is strangely supposed that such an elimination of the distinction of nature and mind is the logical result of the idealistic conception of the absolute. When it is maintained that there can be no abstract separation of mind and nature, subject and

object, it is argued that mind and nature are identified, and hence it is said that we must fall back upon a unity which is manifested indifferently in both. This objection seems to me to rest upon a misconception of what Idealism affirms. What is really maintained is that the conception of nature as an independent reality is a conception which, if taken in its strict sense, contradicts itself. If nature is an independent reality, it can have in it no principle of unity. For the highest principle by which it can be determined is that of the interdependence of its parts, and this principle still leaves the parts external to one another, while it explains the process of nature as the changes which are produced in each part by the action upon it of the others. But such a conception does not take us beyond the idea of an aggregate of parts only externally or mechanically related to one another. On the other hand, when mind is separated from nature, it can only be conceived as an abstract unity which, as having no differences within itself, must for ever remain in its abstractness. Now Idealism refuses to admit that nature and mind are thus separated. It regards nature as the manifestation of mind, and mind as the principle of unity implied in nature. Hence, for the mechanical conception of nature as a system of interdependent parts undergoing correspondent changes, is substituted the organic idea of nature as a system which develops towards an end. This view transforms the conception of nature, not by denying that it is a system, but by regarding it as a system which is rational, and therefore is intelligible to all beings in whom reason operates. Now, if we have to interpret nature from the point of view of reason, the key to nature is to be found in mind. Hence the absolute cannot be adequately conceived merely as the unity which is beyond the distinction of nature and mind, but only as the unity which is implicit in nature and explicit in mind. When, therefore, we seek to determine the relation of particular forms of being to the absolute, the question is how far each is the explicit manifestation of rationality. No form of reality can be regarded as " mere appearance," but only as the more or less adequate manifestation of the principle which is the source and explanation of all reality. When, therefore, we speak of an "individual" reality, we must remember that its individuality is constituted by its relation to the whole. On the other hand, an individual reality cannot be defined as nothing but the sum of its relations to other individual realities. The conception of reality as determined purely by the relations of one thing to another overlooks the principle of unity which is present in all alike. This is true even of inorganic things. Each atom of oxygen or hydrogen is nothing apart from its relations, but each participates in the universal, so that an atom of each is always determined by the relations into which it is capable of entering, while yet it manifests the character peculiar to all atoms of its own kind. The individuality in this case is of a very simple character. Much more obvious is the principle of individuality in the case of living beings, which do not persist in the same unchangeable relations, but exhibit a whole series of relations to the environment. Hence we can only describe the nature of a living being by pointing out the cycle of changes through which it passes. The living being is thus distinguished from the non-living by the greater complexity of its relations, and by the more express exhibition of its individual unity. But it is especially in self-conscious beings that individuality and universality reach their higher stage. Speaking generally, we must therefore say that a being is more truly individual, the more perfectly it contains within itself the principle of the whole. We cannot therefore say that the absolute is manifested equally in all beings; indeed, strictly speaking, it is only in self-conscious beings that the true nature of the absolute is revealed. Now, if it is true that only as reason is developed in a being does it express what is the true principle of the whole, it is manifest that the absolute cannot be realised, as it truly is, in beings lower than man, and that even in man it is not realised in its absolute completeness. By this conception of the immanence of the absolute in all forms of being, together with the recognition that in man at his best the absolute is most fully manifested, we are enabled to see that the conception of the absolute as merely the unchanging substance which persists in all forms of changing existence is quite inadequate. Such a conception, on the one hand, abolishes all the distinctions of one being from another, making them all equally unreal; and, on the other hand, it denies that the absolute is a self-revealing subject, immanent in all forms of being, but manifested truly only in those that are self-conscious.

(2) The absolute is inadequately conceived when it is defined as the power which is manifested in all particular forms of reality, or, in other words, simply as the first cause or creator of the world. The conception of power or force is that of a negative activity which manifests itself in overcoming some other power which is opposed to it. The mechanical conception of energy is the "power of doing work," and is always explained as manifested in opposition to that which resists it. All energy is therefore by its very nature

limited. When, therefore, we speak of infinite power, we virtually transcend the conception of energy, for "infinite" power must be the energy which includes in itself all forms of energy. Such a conception takes us beyond the conception of power altogether. The only kind of power which can be called infinite is that power which is self-determinant, and such a power is found only in self-conscious energy, which is truly infinite because it returns upon itself or preserves its unity in all its manifestations. In self-conscious energy, object and subject are identical. In man this energy of self-consciousness is not complete, because man is not completely self-conscious. But in the absolute there must be complete self-consciousness. Now, if we are compelled to conceive of the absolute as complete self-consciousness, there is in the absolute the perfect unity of subject and object. And as such a unity admits of no degrees, there can be no absolute origination of reality, for this would mean the absolute origination of some phase of the absolute. The ordinary conception of creation as the origination of the world out of nothing conveys a truth in the form of a self-contradiction: it expresses the idea of self-determining activity in the imaginative form of a transition from nothing to reality as taking place in time. A blank nothing is imagined, which is at bottom merely the abstraction from all determinate reality, and then it is imagined that this blank nothing is succeeded by determinate reality. The conception of causality, as it is employed in determining the relation of one phase of reality to another, is transferred to the relation between the absolute and determinate reality. Now, as we have seen, the conception of causal connexion has no meaning except as expressing the dependence of particular phases of reality upon one another, and ultimately we are compelled to recognise that such interdependence of particular phases of reality presupposes a self-determining principle. When we have reached this point of view, we have transcended the category of causality, and it is therefore inadmissible to employ it in seeking to explain the relation of the parts to the whole. But this is what is done in the ordinary conception of creation, though the inadequacy of the conception is virtually admitted when the creation of the world is figured as the origination of it from nothing. For "nothing" is represented as if it were a material to which a definite form was given by the action upon it of an external cause. It is obvious that this crude way of conceiving the relation of the world to the absolute must be discarded. The world cannot be separated from the absolute, but must be regarded as the manifestation or objectification of the absolute, or, in other words, as the absolute itself regarded in its abstract opposition to itself. This opposition, however, is merely a distinction; for that which is opposed to the absolute is the absolute itself.

(3) The absolute is not adequately conceived as a person, although no doubt the conception of personality is much more adequate as a predicate of the absolute than that of power. By a "person" we mean a being that is an individual, and, further, an individual who is capable of conceiving himself as a self. But personality emphasises the ex-

clusive aspect of self-activity, and thus one person is separated from and opposed to another. On this basis of exclusive selfhood all rights are based, a right being the expression of the self in that which has no self. Now, so far as the absolute is affirmed to be a person, the main idea is that the absolute is self-conscious, and to this extent it is true that the absolute is a person. But the absolute is not properly conceived as a person in the sense of being an exclusive self-centred individual. The conception of personality is inadequate even when applied to man, for it is not true that man is merely a person. The first consciousness of exclusive or adverse relations to others must be supplemented by the conception of man as essentially spirit, that is, as a being whose true self is found in relation to what is not self. Man is therefore not adequately conceived as an exclusive self, but only as a self whose true nature is to transcend his exclusiveness and to find himself in what seems at first to be opposed to him. In other words, man is essentially self-separative: he must go out of his apparently self-centred life in order to find himself in a truer and richer life. This conception of a self-opposing subject must be applied to the absolute. The absolute is not an abstract person, but a spirit, *i.e.* a being whose essential nature consists in opposing to itself beings in unity with whom it realises itself. This conception of a self-alienating or self-distinguishing subject seems to me the fundamental idea which is expressed in the doctrine of the Trinity. We can conceive nothing higher than a self-conscious subject, who, in the infinite fulness of his nature, exhibits his perfection in beings who realise themselves in identification with him. What Schiller expresses in a figurative way seems to me to be the necessary result of philosophy:—

> "Freundlos war der grosse Weltenmeister,
> Fühlte Mangel, darum schuf er Geister,
> Sel'ge Spiegel seiner Seligkeit.
> Fand das höchste Wesen schon kein Gleiches,
> Aus dem Kelch des ganzen Wesenreiches
> Schäumt ihm die Unendlichkeit."

There is at present a tendency to maintain that the absolute must be defined as something higher than a self-conscious subject. This view seems to me to rest upon the false assumption that the distinction of subject and object is a mark of limitation. But it can only be a mark of limitation on the supposition that the object is in some way disparate from the subject, *i.e.* contains an element which is incomprehensible. The view which is here maintained is that, in the absolute, subject and object are absolutely identical; in other words, that the subject is its own object. If it is objected that in that case there is no distinction between them, the answer is that as the subject comprehends all reality, there is in the absolute no distinction *between* subject and object, but there is an infinity of distinctions *within* the absolute. The absolute, in other words, is essentially self-distinguishing.

It has already been maintained that the world, as the manifestation of God, is purposive. It must be observed, however, that this purpose is not something superadded to the world, but is implied in its very nature. It is important to make this observation, because the whole objection to the teleological view of the world arises from confusing mechanical with immanent teleology. The idealistic view is therefore hostile to the conception of Providence as the external adaptation of events to an end. Mr. Balfour tells us that one cannot "think of evolution in a God-created world without attributing to its Author the notion of purpose slowly worked out."* It is of course obvious that the conception of God implies that the process of evolution is towards an end; but this process cannot be adequately described as a "preferential exercise of divine power." We cannot conceive of the world as first created, and then directed towards an end. The reality of the world implies the continuous self-determination of God, and this self-determination involves the process by which the world is maintained as an organic whole. We cannot, therefore, separate the evolution of the world from its existence. If we do so, we fall into the difficulty urged by Kant against the argument from design, that we

* *Foundations of Belief*, p. 328.

presuppose a "matter" to which the divine Architect gives shape. Such a "matter" is unthinkable. The nearest approach we can make to it is in some such conception as that of the primitive matter from which, according to the nebular theory, the complex forms of our solar system have been evolved. But in this nebulous matter there is already implied the "promise and potency" of all forms of life, and hence it can only be called "matter" in the relative sense of being a less developed form of the world than is realised in the subsequent stages of evolution. The purpose, then, which must be affirmed is not externally added to the world, but is already implied in the very existence of the world. The world is an organic whole, in which each part exists and has its proper nature only in and through the others. Hence the evolution from lower to higher forms is not a matter of accident, but is inseparable from the existence of the world. A distinction, however, must be drawn between different orders of being. It is only in the case of man that we can speak not only of evolution, but of conscious evolution or progress. The scientific doctrine of evolution has enabled us to see that the law of all finite forms of being is a law of development; in other words, that the real is not the actual as it first appears in time, but the ideal which is implicit in the actual, and which is present in it as the active principle determining the process in which it is manifested. In the case of beings lower than man this process does not reach the stage of a self-conscious development; or, at least, even the highest animals have only an indefinite consciousness of self, and, therefore, can hardly be said to be capable of ideals. Man, however, not only develops, but he is capable of grasping the law of his own development, and, therefore, of contrasting with his immediate self an ideal of himself in which is embodied his conception of what he ought to be, as distinguished from what he is. This capability of returning upon himself and setting up ideals is the fundamental condition of human progress. The ideal, however, while it is contrasted with the actual, is never in contradiction to the actual; it is but the actual grasped in its ideal nature, as that end towards which all prior development has been striving. Were it otherwise, the progress of man would be impossible. It is thus obvious that, on the one hand, progress consists in conformity to the purpose which is involved in the whole nature of things, and, on the other hand, that this purpose can be realised only through the free activity of man. The spiritual life of man cannot be imparted to him from without; it consists in the conscious realisation of the ideal. It is, therefore, a very inadequate conception of life which is expressed in the formula that there is a "Power not ourselves which makes for righteousness." The "Power" which makes for righteousness is the conscious willing of righteousness, *i.e.* the conception and realisation of the meaning of the world. It is true that righteousness can be realised only because it is the true law of man's being; but it is a law which operates only in and through his self-conscious life.

It is, then, the very nature of all finite

forms of being that their reality consists in a process by which they come to be what in idea they are. In the case of man, whose development is a self-conscious process, the development of goodness consists in the transcendence of his immediate or natural life. So far as the life of man is merely natural, he is neither good nor evil; it is only because he is capable of abstracting from the immediate life of feeling that he is moral. And with this capacity is bound up the possibility of willing evil. The question as to the existence of evil has been obscured by the manner in which the problem has been put. The church fathers, conceiving of man as independently created, maintained that he was originally perfect in wisdom and holiness, and that evil was introduced into the world by the sin of the first man. It need hardly be said that this explanation not only explains nothing, but is self-contradictory and out of harmony with all that we know of primitive man. It explains nothing, because moral evil cannot be externally transferred from one person to another; the very idea of moral evil being that it proceeds from a free act. It is self-contradictory, because a perfect being could have no disposition to will evil. And it is incompatible with the results of scientific discovery, which make it certain that primitive man began at the lowest and not the highest stage. The state of perfection ascribed to primitive man is, therefore, the goal and not the starting-point of humanity. Man was, therefore, in his original state evil, in the sense that evil is inseparable from the life of a being who can attain to good only through freedom, which involves the freedom to fall into error and evil. The original state of man was one in which he had the most inadequate conception of the world, himself, and God. The progress of man has involved a continual struggle with the cruder ideal of an earlier age. The spiritual life is not a primitive endowment, but the result of long-continued pain and travail. Evil is not an accident; it is inseparable from the process by which man transcends his immediate life. It is only through the experience of evil that man has obtained a consciousness of the depths as well as the heights of his nature. On the other hand, the process of human life has been a continual transcendence of evil. The desire of man is for goodness and God, and his experience that evil is in contradiction to his true self makes it impossible for him to rest in it. Hence even at the earliest stage man is never absolutely evil; he hates his enemy, it is true, but he sacrifices his natural impulses, and even his life, for his family or tribe. Thus the imperfect development of his moral life is the counterpart of his imperfect knowledge of himself.

The deliverance of man from the evil which belongs to his nature, as a being whose life is a process, is possible only through the comprehension of himself as in his ideal nature identical with God. The mediæval conception of salvation cannot be accepted in the form in which it is stated. Man, it was argued, might conceivably have been liberated from sin in two ways: either God might have pardoned him out of pure mercy, or man might have expiated his sin by a humility correspondent to the magnitude of his guilt. But the former, it was held, conflicts with the justice of God; and the latter is impossible, because man could not undergo a humiliation proportionate to the self-assertion implied in disobedience to the will of God. Hence God offered up his Son in man's stead, thus reconciling infinite justice with infinite mercy.

It is impossible to state this highly artificial doctrine without seeing that it is the product of conflicting ideas which are not properly reconciled with each other. The starting-point is the conception of personal sin, one of the central ideas of Christianity. Sin is then identified with crime, and therefore God is conceived as an inexorable judge. But sin is not crime, nor can God be regarded as a judge. Crime is a violation of the personal rights of another; it is an offence against the external order of the state, which must be expiated by an external punishment. Sin, on the other hand, is not a violation of rights, but a desecration of the ideal nature of the sinner, the willing of himself as in his essence he is not. Hence sin requires no external punishment to bring it home to the sinner: it brings its own punishment with it in the destruction of the higher life, the realisation of which is blessedness. In man, by virtue of the divine principle in him, the consciousness of God is bound up with the consciousness of himself, and he cannot do violence to the one without doing violence to the other. Hence God is not a judge, allotting punishment according to an external law, but the perfectly holy Being, by reference to whom man condemns himself. No external punishment can transform the inner nature. The criminal, after undergoing punishment, may be more hardened in crime than ever, and yet society must punish him, because its function is to preserve the social bond, which by his act the criminal has assailed. But religion has in view not the preservation of social order, but the regeneration of the individual: it deals with the inner nature of man, not with the result of his act upon society; and hence, unless it transforms and spiritualises him, it entirely fails of its end.

The sin of Adam, according to the mediæval theory, consisted in pride, or the attempt to equalise himself with God. The truth implied in this view is that in so far as man seeks to realise his true self in separation from God, and therefore in willing his own good in isolation from the good of his fellowmen, he brings upon himself spiritual death. But this truth is obscured by the vulgar notion that sin is the attempt of man to equalise himself with God,—a notion obviously based upon the conception of God as a Ruler whose majesty must be asserted. This pagan conception, drawn mainly from the idea of Cæsar, as the representative of order and law, is entirely foreign to the Christian idea of God. Even Plato saw that "in God there can be no envy;" and mediæval thinkers themselves virtually deny this false conception of God, when they speak of the incarnation as an expression of the infinite love of God. Here, in fact, we come upon the only purely Christian idea in the whole doctrine. Stripped of its artificial form, what is affirmed is that it is the very nature of

God to communicate himself to finite beings; that, loving his creatures with an infinite love, he can realise his own blessedness only in them. Man can therefore be saved from sin only as he realises in his own life the self-communicating spirit of God. In taking upon himself the burden of the race, he lives a divine life. This is the secret which Jesus realised in his life, and to have made this secret practically our own is to be justified by faith.

The Christian ideal of life, as here understood, is broad enough to embrace all the elements which in their combination constitute the complex spirit of the modern world. Every advance in science is the preparation for a fuller and clearer conception of God; every improvement in the organisation of society is a further development of that community of free beings by which the ideal of an organic unity of humanity is in process of realisation; every advance in the artistic interpretation of the world helps to individualise the idea of the organic unity by which all things are bound together. The ideal of the Church has tended to limit Christianity to the direct promotion of the moral ideal, to the exclusion of the more comprehensive ideal which recognises that the goal is the full development of all the means by which the full perfection of humanity is realised. The Christian ideal, as embodied in the teaching of Jesus, was free from this limitation. It saw God in the orderly processes of nature and in the beauty of the world, as well as in the loving service of humanity. In principle it therefore embraced all that makes for the higher life. The Christianity of our day must free itself from the narrow conception of life by which Protestantism has tended to limit its principle. It must recognise that the ideal of Christian manhood includes within it the Greek ideal of clear thought and the love of beauty, as well as the Jewish ideal of righteousness, and the Roman ideal of law and order, harmonising all by the divine spirit of love to God and man, on the basis of that free spirit which has come to us mainly from our Teutonic ancestors.

www.ingramcontent.com/pod-product-compliance
Lightning Source LLC
Chambersburg PA
CBHW021404230426
43666CB00006B/637